Mother
Love

Mother
Love

Stories about
Births, Babies & Beyond

Edited by Debra Adelaide

RANDOM HOUSE
AUSTRALIA

Random House Australia Pty Ltd
20 Alfred Street, Milsons Point, NSW 2061

Sydney New York Toronto
London Auckland Johannesburg
and agencies throughout the world

First published in 1996

National Library of Australia
Cataloguing-in-Publication data:

Motherlove
ISBN 0 09 183131 8.

1. Love, Maternal–Literary collections. 2. Australian
prose literature–20th century. 3. Australian prose
literature–Women authors. I. Adelaide, Debra, 1958– .

A828.308080354

Cover photograph by Lesley O'Donnell
Designed by Mary Callahan
Typeset in 11.5/15.5 Goudy by Midland Typesetters, Maryborough
Printed and bound by Griffin Paperbacks, Adelaide

Anna Maria Dell'oso's 'Harvest Day' was first published in *Cats,
Cradles and Chamomile* Tea (Random House: 1989); an earlier version
of 'Happy Birthday' by Julie Clarke was first published in *HQ* magazine
(Autumn: 1993).

Lines from Sylvia Plath's 'Nick and the Candlestick' are from *Ariel* (1965)
published by Faber & Faber, and are reproduced with permission.

10 9 8 7 6 5 4 3

for
Joseph and Ellen

Contents

Introduction 1

MARY MOODY
Catching the Baby 11

BRENDA WALKER
All the Points of the Compass 25

FIONA PLACE
Apocalypse Now 43

ANNETTE STEWART
'Cover Lightly, Gentle Earth' 71

NONI HAZLEHURST
Babies and Beyond 83

RACHEL WARD
Milk Fever 93

SARA DOWSE
Connections around Childbirth 109

ANNA BOOTH
Balancing Act 123

SUE WOOLFE
Ghosts 133

ADELE HORIN
The Secret Circle 167

GABRIELLE CAREY
Prenatal Depression, Postmodern World 179

PAT MAMAJUN TORRES
Mowangka's Birth 199

DEBRA ADELAIDE
Desiring the Unknown 211

MONICA TRAPAGA
Gardening and Giving Birth 227

DOROTHY JOHNSTON
A Christmas Story 235

JULIE CLARKE
Happy Birthday 251

ANNA MARIA DELL'OSO
Harvest Day 273

Notes on Contributors 303

My little girl was born at 20 minutes past 7. I was seventeen hours ill; the last eight being exquisite agony. Pain will always be a matter of comparison now; I believe I should be able to smile over a trifling matter like having a limb sawn slowly off.

Ethel Turner, *The Diaries of Ethel Turner* ([1898], 1979)

Henny thought, 'I like a baby's room best: there are no books, no lead, no nonsense,' and she thought of evenings when she had come in to see the usual sight, a baby's head lying sideways, the eyes closed, the fine dark hair growing thicker over the thin-skinned oval skull, the little nightgown frill, the eyes closed, and one fist clenched on the pillow. She pulled the edge of the blanket straight thoughtfully, 'A mother! What are we worth really? They all grow up whether you look after them or not.'

Christina Stead, *The Man Who Loved Children* (1940)

You are the one
Solid the spaces lean on, envious.
You are the baby in the barn.

Sylvia Plath, 'Nick and the Candlestick' ([1962], 1965)

DEBRA ADELAIDE

Introduction

Who has held the naked foot of a baby and not marvelled at its miniature perfection, its gentle warmth, its lingering softness? Who has traced a finger up that delicate quilted sole and not been moved by the beauty, the vulnerability, the incipient strength and mobility?

Few of us. A baby has the capacity to steal the heart of even the stoniest.

Yet who has ever talked or written of such things without feeling self-conscious, out of place, ridiculous, or plain *soppy*?

One day I looked at my bookshelves and wondered why this was so, wondered why there was so little on this topic. There was the odd story in a collection or two, a few poems I remembered reading from years back. But

1

nothing much else. There were lots of novels, poems, stories, and even plays about *relationships* from every possible angle, but the relationship which was conspicuously missing was that of the mother and her child, and especially her baby. Human relationships are the staple of literature. Lovers write about their partners, husbands about their wives, grown-up children about their mothers and fathers, women about their secret lovers—the list goes on and on, but it ends somewhere before we get to the peculiarly uncomfortable topic of how a *mother feels about her baby*.

Of course there are plenty of baby books—manuals, handbooks, infant care books, child psychology guides, books on giving birth, home birth, hospital care, magazines for parents, for parents-to-be, even books on having twins and preparatory diaries to take a woman day by day through a pregnancy.

But all these books, as valuable as they may be in their different ways, do not tell the real story of what it is like to be pregnant, give birth, handle a baby and raise a child. The real story, as anyone who has had a child knows, involves a lot more blood, dreams, tears, laughter and screams than the authorities are prepared to reveal. Birth and babies are compelling topics. For a writer, the instinct to write about one's birth or one's child—often the most compelling experience of one's life—is immensely strong. But usually the urge to suppress it overrides this instinct, because the messages one receives say: Don't write about this. It's self-indulgent. Boring. Only of limited interest. Not the stuff of genuine literature. Forget it. Well, write it, then, but send it to a parents' publication. Or one of those *women's* magazines.

So what is the real story about having a baby? And can just one book presume to offer it? Well, for a start, whatever the real story might be, *Motherlove* shows that despite a new mother's eagerness for knowledge (and despite the information to be gleaned from all those baby books), after the event a new mother comes to understand she knows nothing.

Because no one has talked about how it would be a love affair. The maternal bond has often been mentioned, but no one has explained just how strong that bond is; how, in those first weeks or months, it might be literally impossible for a mother to be away from her baby. How she might carry her from room to room, and refuse to go out even for an hour. How all she'd want—in between the feeding, the washing, the nappy-folding (all that she'd read about)—all she'd want to do would be to lie beside her baby, hold her, smell her, and gaze adoringly at the creature that is flesh of her flesh, blood of her blood.

No one, for sure, admitted a mother might want breastfeeding as much as her baby, or hinted that weaning might make *her* sad, not her baby, that her body might cry *tears of milk*, while the baby thrived at the bottle.

No one explained she would sleep with all her senses

on alert, so that even if her baby was a *good sleeper*, she would wake at the slightest sound: a muffled rasp of the new cotton bassinet sheets against the blanket. At a sigh or whimper as faint as a newborn rabbit's. At the creak of the wicker basket that had held many babies, including herself.

No one suggested a new mother would really *desire* to stay home and adore her most brilliant achievement, and selfishly hold onto those brief moments when she was someone else's complete and utter source of support. It had never felt so great to be needed.

Nor so terrifying.

Motherhood, like giving birth, is an amazing thing. On the one hand it is all so common. So ordinary we don't feel the need to talk about it, or educate the next generation into it. And yet everyone's experience is unique. Every birth experience is a phenomenon. Every mark of the birth a different shape or texture. Every child an individual, even in the womb. Every baby born an absolute miracle.

And despite the utter commonness of this experience, it is still, in certain contexts, taboo to discuss these aspects of children, babies, and births, or even to acknowledge their existence. The task I set the contributors was with this in mind. It was time, I thought, to break some taboos. If it was indulgent, I thought, well and good. If it was emotional and soppy, even better. Let's get emotional for a change. Let's indulge ourselves with some birth stories, some descriptions of fierce, powerful baby-worship. And let's spice it with a bit of blood and guts, and finally leaven it with a touch of humour.

Of course the contributors to *Motherlove* responded to this challenge in vastly different ways. What has intrigued me as editor is to see how each of these pieces reveals a new and separate facet of the same jewel. Each of them shows that although the process of having a baby is the same, the *story* is always a unique one. Even those pieces which are fairly detailed descriptions of births prove that the experience is different, again and again. What remains the same are a few details: for instance, a newborn baby smelling *like freshly baked bread*. Or the belief that at the heart of the birth experience lies the ineffable: that *there is no word for it.*

But some authors have wrestled with words to describe the indescribable: the extraordinary moment when a woman holds her baby for the very first time, which is *like two lovers seeing each other after a long separation*. The moment immediately after the birth, when only a few things make sense, but one of them is that a woman's body has *just performed the most extraordinary miracle*, the other that she will *never be the same again*.

As this book took shape and the contributors were drawn in, the commission to upset the taboos broadened and the boundaries, such as they were, took on a fuzzy shapelessness. The idea, for instance, of celebrating the sumptuous aspects of being a mother, of writing about the sensuousness of the relationship between mother and child, expanded enormously. Write about any aspect, I had said to the contributors, of pregnancy, birth, babies, or being a mother of young children. Write whatever you like: a story or an autobiographical piece. Out of those wild and loose 'instructions' has come this mixture of fact, excursive prose, autobiography, fiction, essay, fantasy, and even a few pieces of poetry.

Some contributors were unable to write 'birth' stories, but wanted to write about the 'beyond' or even the 'before'. Some were compelled to write about death, as well as birth, about the realisation of fears, as much as the fulfilment of dreams. In some of these stories, the arrival of a child fractures relationships, so for instance the tidy trinity of the family becomes a burden, or a dream, while the new mother struggles on alone with her baby. There are pieces which describe how a birth—being *a matter of life and death*—may not always be a moment of triumph, but a time when one's *dreams and hopes end*, a time when *the promise of a new life* may be unfulfilled.

There are writings about terrors and nightmares, as well as about rhapsodic pleasures and sensual delights. There are stories about the pull of the workforce, about work not being an income-earning occupation, but a *refuge*, an irresistible and necessary counter to home life. There are stories about the tug of another culture, another country, where the pressures involved in having a baby are negligible, and where an expectant mother has *nothing more urgent to do than sew and cook*. There are pieces which mourn or regret the loss of life, as well as the passing of a *lifestyle*, but these are also invariably the same pieces in which a *million reasons* might be offered for the change which has brought this extraordinary *gift of a child*.

We have pieces describing the *apocalyptic* intensity of the pain, and the impossibility of forgetting. There are pieces describing the vast differences in birth management, from the interventionist hospital procedure, where a mother has *never felt such fright and desolation*, to the quiet birth at home, a family affair where the same mother now hands her grown daughter her own first-born child: this becomes *the most exquisite moment* of her life. Another author, now a grandmother, has *come to see childbirth as a central, revelatory event* in life, and asks questions about the significance of the birth experience in the context of culture and nationhood.

So the real story, as *Motherlove* shows, is as diverse as it is powerful; as confronting as it is compelling. It is, as I said, about the blood and guts of giving birth. The disappointments, the fears, the confusion and sense of betrayal, even the *horror, the horror*. It's about how really bad the pain is: like *cutting off your own leg*, or like being *blown apart*, or *erupting*, like *Mount Vesuvius resides inside*, not a baby. And also about how and why, knowing this, you're prepared to undergo that *pain* again. It's about the emotions which take you on a journey faster than the speed of light as you swing from the last overwhelming burning *pain*, to the elation of holding your baby for the *very first time*.

And it's about being so fallible, so human. About gritting your teeth in the face of torturous fatigue or harassment. About the hopes cherished that the arrival of a new baby will heal wounds, repair rifts, and about how such hopes can be vain. It's about learning to be *a proper mother*, because the role doesn't necessarily come naturally, and discovering that no one can tell you what *a proper mother* really is.

On the lighter (but no less compelling) side, some of these pieces are about untold stories, of the secret lives of mothers of young children, whose daily *odyssey from bed to desk* is an untold epic of achievement and survival. Working mothers, it's revealed, form a *female underground of unsung heroes, toiling invisibly in order to get to work on time*.

And the story, above all, is a continuing one. This collection emphasises in various ways, and in different pieces, the interconnectedness of the birth experience. Some of the birth stories begin a generation or two earlier. Some narrators can't write about the child, alone. Some must begin with the *grandmother* or even the *grandmother's ghost*. Or they ask, where does the story begin—*with his birth? his conception? his parents' first meeting . . . ?*

Behind the creation of all collections and anthologies there is a hidden story, replayed everywhere with variations: authors stretching deadlines to impossible limits; rejection by the editor; failure of stories to materialise despite numerous promises; anguish that the author hasn't been able to write the piece she or he wanted, and would x, y or z from the bottom drawer 'do' instead? And, inevitably, the collection inventing and reinventing itself far and away beyond the original idea. But what sets *Motherlove* apart from other collections is the fact that all the authors here are mothers first, and most of them are still mothers of young children. The writing, in this case, can never come first. Many of the pieces here reflect the packed yet utterly fragmented life of the contemporary mother; the one performing several jobs and with several children, whose method of writing has to be a matter of stealing half an hour here, another hour there, gradually assembling a piece, stretching the deadline, and trusting the whole will be okay.

It is an immense pleasure to read through these pieces again and again and know that yes, this is all okay. To see that this fragmentation can be its own special story. And to know that each piece has its individual stamp, because each, whether fiction or autobiography, essay or excursion, is from the heart of the mother, and written from the instinct that we call *motherlove*.

MARY MOODY
Catching the Baby

The days and weeks of my life have passed almost unnoticed. Was it yesterday that I stood stirring porridge, with three small children at my heels? And now, somehow, I'm standing at the stove, still wielding a wooden spoon, but with my grandson on my hip.

Looking in the mirror I see the signs of age. The carrot-colour is fading from my hair, the freckles, no longer prominent, now merging with the lines that will deepen, again with age.

I can't take my eyes off my grandson who is playing on the floor. He crawls to me, then stretches out his arms to be lifted up. My heart lurches with love, the same love I felt for his mother more than twenty years ago. There are occasional flashes of her at the same age. The look of concentration as he plays. The dreamy stare when he's in a trance. But his smile, his belly laugh and his adventurous spirit are all his own.

I was young and foolish when I conceived my first child, Miriam. She was planned, unlike the two brothers who followed after.

It's delicious planning to make a baby. It gives the act of lovemaking a totally different perspective; conspiratorial and exciting. Even now I can't imagine what I was thinking about. Plunging into motherhood with so little trepidation. My career had just begun, and there was no thought (or possibility) of marriage. Then, as now, I quite enjoyed the shock value of breaking with convention.

I worked until a few weeks before she was due, keeping busy and cobbling together the basic requirements with very little money. A cradle, two dozen nappies and some Viyella nighties. My mother, of course, knitted furiously.

There was not much to read about birth in those days, except Grantly Dick-Read (*Childbirth Without Fear*) and some ante-natal texts prepared by the hospital physio staff. I waddled along to some classes and learned basic relaxation techniques, but failed to inveigle my partner, David, into getting involved with the birth. He was 'too old', 'too scared' and 'too inadequate' to help. The thought of the delivery room, the white gowns and the inevitable blood repelled him. There was no point forcing the issue. A reluctant birth helper is no help at all.

My visits to the obstetrician were short and sweet. In

the door, up on the table, how are you feeling? and then out again before I had time to draw breath. He seemed unconcerned that I continued smoking, although he mentioned the risk of a low birth weight baby. Indeed, he seemed more preoccupied with weight gain than smoking, and congratulated me each month when I had only put on a little weight. In those days, it seems, getting fat during pregnancy was more frowned upon than puffing on a fag. He warned me how difficult it would be to 'get my figure back afterwards' if I packed on the pounds.

A glowing picture of health throughout the pregnancy, towards the end I developed cystitis, with raging fevers and burning urine. There was a risk, I was told, of harm to the baby. So an induction was organised. Much safer to 'deliver' when there is total control, rather than waiting to risk a second bout of sickness. These days, of course, I would have taken a different course of action. Then, I had total trust and faith in the system.

It was a short, intense labour, and for most of the time I was quite alone. The midwives, friendly and efficient, took observations every thirty minutes and hurried away to attend mysterious and sometimes noisy labouring women in adjoining rooms. I managed to cope with the pain of the contractions, coming faster and faster, but I was totally dismayed at the mess I was creating in my wake. When I tried to stand and walk for a moment, unassisted, the floor would be awash with amniotic fluid and splashes of blood. I used paper towels to clean behind me as I walked, hoping the nurses wouldn't observe the growing pile of rubbish in the corner bin. I was enveloped by a peculiar smell, quite distinct from the disinfectant-clean smell of the ward, and it worried me a lot. I was determined not to cause any fuss or to make a noise, but at times I longed to call out for help, or scream as the contractions became more intense.

So many internal examinations. So many mutterings and entries on the chart. The leading midwife informed me that I had made good progress, but that I should have some pethidine now, to get me through until the end of the first stage. She was brusque when I said I thought I could battle on without it. 'You'll be sorry later on,' she muttered in dire warning.

I was lucky in so many ways. The labour was rapid and uneventful. I began to feel a strong urge to push, and used the buzzer for the first time. 'Not yet,' they said. 'It's your first.' Then they went away to leave me fighting against this overwhelming sensation, over which I had no control. Disobediently I pushed with three or four contractions, until I felt a stretching, burning feeling between my legs. I buzzed again, for the last time.

Panic all around. The baby had almost crowned. Just time to slide on the green leg covers and strap my feet to the stirrups. No time for the doctor to get back from his rooms full of expectant women. Two more pushes and the stinging was over, followed by a small push and the most wonderful wet slippery feeling.

Miriam breathed spontaneously but didn't cry. Self-contained, even then!

Although young and quite naive, I believed I had prepared well for this moment. I'd read, exercised, laid out clothes and blankets for the homecoming, rubbed cream on my nipples and massaged my stretching belly. Nothing had prepared me for the way I felt when I gathered Miriam into my arms, and saw her small, perfect face for the first time. I don't actually think there is a word that can capture this feeling.

I didn't feel tired, or sore, or sorry. I felt the most amazing burst of energy, and wanted to run out onto the highway and stop every car and every person in the street, and do high kicks, and dance on tabletops. The nurses wanted me to rest, to sleep, to recover. How could I? David came in, looking drained and exhausted. He quickly tuned into my excitement, and experienced some of the elation for himself. I think he and my mother went out and got drunk!

They took Miriam away half an hour after the birth. I was told I could see her again for a feed at four pm. It was only 1.30 in the afternoon, so I had a long wait ahead of me. I had not put her to the breast in the labour room as it was not encouraged. A lot of time was spent scrubbing her clean and weighing her—she was indeed a low birth weight as a result of being induced several weeks early, and of course from my smoking. She was nothing but skin and bone, but exquisite in my eyes. A young nurse, younger than me, brought her down to the ward precisely at four o'clock. She helped Miriam to 'latch on' to my nipple, which she did with tremendous enthusiasm. It was the first time I cried, tears of joy, and the young nurse cried too.

I didn't come down for days or weeks. In fact, I don't think I ever came down again. This was what being alive was all about, for me. This love, this happiness, this sense of purpose and fulfilment. I had my terrible moments, of course, usually over the washing tub, trying to separate sticky globs of shit from the nappies and clothing. Miriam slept through the night in no time and I weaned her and returned to work when she was seven weeks old (how could I?), leaving her with a friend who had two boisterous children, Miriam's instant family. We were happy, and I believed implicitly that my birth had been a huge success; a triumph, a miracle. I proudly announced to friends and neighbours that in sexual terms, women left men standing at the starting gate. Birth was the ultimate in sexual fulfilment. I still believe it to be true.

After Miriam I had two beautiful boys. One a traumatic birth in hospital, the result of an induction that went too fast. A thirty-two minute labour and a bruised-about-the-head newborn. It took Aaron months, probably years, to recover fully from the shock of his precipitous entry into the world.

According to the dates he was overdue and although I

desperately wanted a natural start to labour, I agreed to allow the doctor to break my waters to get things going. It's a weird feeling, not painful but strange, when the small, sharp hook punctures the membrane at the cervix, and the flood of warm fluid washes out between your legs, revealing the outline of the baby against the skin of your belly. I thought my contractions would start spontaneously, but they didn't. All morning I sat twiddling my thumbs, waiting for labour to begin. At lunchtime the doctor popped in and said I would have to have a oxytocin drip to establish labour. It was dangerous, he said; now that the membranes had been ruptured, the womb was open to the risk of infection.

The drip went in and within two minutes I experienced my first contraction. In fact, the entire short labour was really one long contraction because the flow of the drip was too fast. Within half an hour my cervix dilated and two strong pushes produced the baby. He was covered with vernix and had no subcutaneous fat, indicating that he was not overdue at all, but in fact three or more weeks premature. He breathed without assistance but was very blue from oxygen deprivation during the labour. The baby needs those breaks between contractions to get its oxygen supply, and there had been virtually no breaks at all. His head was badly bruised, and he was taken away within ten minutes to be revived in a humidicrib.

I have never felt such fright and desolation. I pleaded to be allowed to go with him to the premmie nursery, but it was not allowed. I was told to sleep and recover. I could see him after the evening meal. It was only lunchtime, and I couldn't imagine how I could wait that long. I simply lay in the delivery room and sobbed until they took me down to the ward. Against strict instructions I took a lift to the third floor and found Aaron in his crib. Lying on his tummy wearing only a nappy, his thin little body had started to turn pink. I had barely seen him in the delivery room, only touched him for a moment before he was whisked away. I put my hands in through the round holes and stroked him. He looked so vulnerable. My heart was filled with guilt and remorse. I felt I was responsible for his pathetic condition, by having the induction which effectively dragged him from his warm growing place and thrust him unwillingly and painfully into the world.

For the first time I saw that by interfering in the natural process of birth, a chain of disasters can so easily happen. Even though Miriam had also been induced, in many ways I had been fortunate with her birth because I had been left to my own devices. My reluctance to cause a fuss, and the uncomplicated nature of the labour, meant that I escaped all sorts of intervention. With Aaron's birth, we hadn't been nearly as fortunate.

Disillusioned, I chose birth at home and a midwife for my third confinement. It was a family affair, and for the first time David was prepared to be involved, although still with some fear and hesitancy. The labour was slow, but steady. It took hours for my cervix to dilate, just about as many hours as it took David to totally support me. The midwife said it was no coincidence. I needed to wait for him before I could move on to the next stage.

Miriam, now aged seven, never left my side for one moment. She was fascinated by the process, peered through her foggy glasses between my legs, and helped by sloshing a wet washer on my face between contractions. It was a bit like being slapped around the face with a wet fish, but I wasn't fazed. She was a vital element of the birth, and I would say nothing to discourage her enthusiasm. I had prepared her and Aaron by talking them through the birth process, and showing them photographs and illustrations of what to expect. Aaron gave up after the baby hadn't appeared within thirty minutes, while Miriam hung in till the end. Until Ethan arrived, eyes open and scowling at the world.

Who can tell if being part of the birth bonds siblings for life? Could there be a different quality in their relationship? Years later, when Miriam was pregnant and planning a home birth herself, she asked if Ethan would like to be her birth supporter. I was invited, and her father too, but she really wanted Ethan there to support her as well. The midwife was quite curious, never having had a fourteen-year-old boy at a birth before. But like all home birth practitioners, she was open to whatever the pregnant mother felt comfortable with. And Miriam, as always, was right.

Miriam read and read through her pregnancy. She approached birth as she would one of her university assignments. In keeping with her academic application, her research was thorough. Initially she planned on a birth centre, but the more she read the more she was convinced to stay at home. There's no Medicare rebate for a home birth; no private insurance coverage. If you want to stay at home, you must be committed enough to outlay up to $2 000, depending on the midwife. So Miriam sold her computer to have the birth she and her partner Richard wanted.

Although excited at the idea of being included in the birth, I was not without some reservations. Most mothers hate to see their children in pain, and over the years I have gone to great lengths to shelter mine from even the mildest hurt. Just normally overprotective. So how would I survive Miriam's pain in labour? Would I shrink from the sight of her agony? What if she couldn't cope, and wanted 'out'?

The labour started ten days early, and got off to an unspectacular start. A few contractions, a spot of blood and some fluid. David was still overseas, having expected the baby to arrive on deadline to fit in with his travel plans. No such luck. Ethan and I dashed to Canberra where Miriam and Richard live, expecting that the labour would hot up during the night. It didn't. Nor the next day or night. Nor the next. So we came home, a three-and-a-half-hour drive, thinking the situation could possibly remain the same for the next two weeks. But of course Miriam's labour began in earnest just an hour after we left Canberra. We arrived home in the mountains, spoke to her on the phone, then turned around and drove all the way back. Nothing like going to a birth scene after seven hours of driving!

The atmosphere inside the little house was cosy and calm when we arrived. The midwife was resting in the dark in the front room, obviously pacing herself for the long night ahead. The labour was well established, with contractions every three minutes, and hot packs were being applied tenderly by Richard. Ethan immediately got involved in helping to apply the heat that helps so much with the pain. At times Miriam seemed to be pushing, but was obviously not quite into transition, so it seemed like the birth was progressing well. She was concentrating hard, but had not yet lost her sense of humour!

We formed a wonderful little team. It was such an intimate atmosphere, and we all worked together to keep Miriam comfortable. We helped her change positions from time to time and worked to keep her spirits up. Richard ran a hot bath and Miriam lay for a while with her eyes closed. I took photographs and kept the water boiling for more hot packs. Ethan held Miriam's hand and talked to her while Richard stroked her and kept the hot packs coming. Every so often the midwife would pop in, see how we were going and leave us to it.

After the bath Miriam announced she didn't want to continue, which is a pretty normal way to feel after five hours of strong labour. I tried to encourage her; Richard reminded her about keeping her body relaxed, which earned him a quick clip around the ears. The midwife suggested that perhaps Miriam would like to go to hospital for an epidural, which was like waving a red rag at a bull. No way. She would walk, and walk she did.

Naked and beautiful Miriam paced the entire length of the house, calling for Richard's support during each contraction. She marched, head up, with a furious expression on her face. Back and forth for twenty minutes, we all kept out of her way. She was walking through transition with all her courage and strength. It was an inspiring sight, and rather than feeling upset at her pain, I felt tremendous pride in her womanliness, her beauty and her inner resources.

Suddenly, she was ready to push. Onto her knees with Richard supporting her arms and head. It was a short second stage, intense but satisfying as the baby's head quickly came on view. At last Miriam appeared to be enjoying herself more, being totally in control. The midwife worked gently to stretch her perineum over the head, slowly, slowly, contraction by contraction. There was intense stinging, I could almost feel it myself, and then Eamonn's head emerged. Before his body was born he breathed spontaneously and let out a small cry, which of course started us all crying with happiness.

The midwife asked if I would like to 'catch' the baby. The term 'deliver' is no longer politically correct, as it implies the skill is with the practitioner rather than with the mother. On the next contraction I would rotate his shoulders, cradle him as his body emerged, then pass him to Miriam, between her legs.

I agreed without hesitation, quickly handed the camera to Ethan and waited for the moment. Eamonn slithered out effortlessly, and we wept as we greeted him. Handing my daughter her first-born child was the most exquisite moment of my life.

Looking back, how can I relate this birth of my grandson with Miriam's own birth twenty-one years ago? There is simply no comparison. Although I experienced all the joy and elation that giving birth brings, I was not enveloped in the warmth and love of my family. I had no partner to touch my skin, or use his hands to massage away the pain. To offer strength and support when nothing else would do. Although I emerged from hospital proud of my achievement, positive about the experience and confident in my ability to cope with motherhood, it says more about my innate personality than the success of the hospital system as it was in the early seventies. Many women emerged shattered from their birth experience, and sadly they continue to do so to this day.

Eamonn's birth was a healing process for me. It helped me to understand more about myself and my relationship with my children. I cannot turn back the clock and change the circumstances of the births of my first two children, but I can go from here with the knowledge that birth can be the most intimate of family experiences. Not an exercise in medical expertise, but an expression of love and trust and support.

Footnote: Eamonn Zachary Parsons was born at 12.30 am on 24 May 1994 after 9½ hours of labour. He weighed 3.6 kg and was 53 cm long.

BRENDA WALKER
All the Points of the Compass

On some maps the compass is drawn as a simple line for true North. Very old or elaborate maps have compasses with many radiant lines, showing gradations of direction.

When I think about my child my memory interrupts itself. I find I cannot write about him simply, as if I were ruling a single line. Where does he begin? At his birth? At his conception? With his parents' first meeting, or in the stories we told each other about our families and ourselves? I can't and don't want to see where he might end.

When I write about him I have to navigate, using many sharp points and half-directions, to show something as complicated, as radiant as simple truth.

I'll begin with his father. I remember how I felt, waiting in the evening for his father.

The house shivers.

The baby and I can feel a tender movement in the house. It's caused by a footstep on the verandah boards. The boards are nailed to unsteady beams below the floor of the room where we wait and wait, six o'clock, reading stories, seven o'clock, a drowsy bottle, listening, seven thirty and there is a ripple in the substance of the house: he's home.

We met because of my Boston lover, who was away in Germany and America researching platelets: things which clump together in the blood.

It happened like this. One evening I talked to the man next to me at the dinner table, some friend of the Boston lover's friends. We had just been introduced. I don't know what we talked about. He remembers that he decided, then, to marry me.

Bertrand Russell was cycling one day when he realised that he didn't love his wife. *Suddenly, as I was riding along a country road, I realised that I no longer loved Alys. I had had no idea until this moment that my love for her was even lessening.* It was the same kind of decisiveness, in reverse. I was very thin, I had black hair to my waist and a white face. I was twenty-one and writing a gloomy PhD. He still wanted to marry me. He didn't mention it. He asked me to a concert instead.

I wore a black dress to the concert and pointy Schiaparelli pink shoes. The shoes' mood won. I decided to spend the night with him.

What was he like? Not shy, not coldly tactical.

I had mail from the Max Plank Institut, in Germany, from Johns Hopkins, in the USA. I'd tear open the envelope to find that the Boston lover hadn't written a word; the page inside was always angry white, except for the official letterhead. The Boston lover sent me blank paper for years. I was writing on Beckett and Céline. Beckett calls love *that desert of loneliness and recrimination.*

We went down a flight of stairs to a basement jeweller. Under the counter there were hundreds of blackened old engagement rings on loops of rope. The one I wanted didn't fit. The dead woman who owned it first was much broader than me. In a while it became mine and I stopped thinking about her hands, how she might have opened her arms to Jesus, at the end, or lifted a bottle of Lysol to her mouth.

The jeweller cut the ring down and cleaned it and charged us thirty dollars.

We lived in a big group house, not a big house, but a big group. The owner thought we were too poor to pay market rent. The cheap rent made it hard to stand up to him. His deaf dog guarded the bathroom against us. At my bedside was a pile of boxes holding a dried dead spider collection, the severed plait of his ex-wife and the letters his great-grandfather wrote home from boarding school. The walls were lined with shelves of crime fiction; I began to read crime fiction here. A kapok mattress, said to be a camp bed from the Boer War, filled the cupboard.

We made our love here and in other cities, behind iron grilles, above the traffic, in places where if the light was angled right, a stranger's message showed in the dust on the surface of a mirror.

I've written two short novels. I've never written about love.

Reviewers have discussed my *sad and chilling fiction*, my *ability to make the words hurt*. My characters are diagnosed in the terms used by self-help books; they are unable to *sustain a lasting relationship*.

So. Love.

From beside the landlord's boxes of spiders and dead hair I watch him work. When he finishes he improvises on an old electric piano with the volume turned well down.

If I drift behind my closed eyes I am back in a saucer chair, a chair exactly like a nest; or a dish for the tongue of a great cat. My mother is playing something rippling and perpetual, making me a covering not of cloth but of warm singing air. I am in a room with him, but I am falling asleep under my mother's hands.

I studied massage properly. I learned about the strong relaxed attachment between muscle and bone. I learned to involve my own hands in this.

We are said to have a connection, through the maternal line, with the ancestors of the Countess Constance Markiewicz, the Irish rebel. In the records a marriage is marked as a split in the line, followed by a clustering of children's names, then further marriages, if they married, and more clusterings. The volume of names can be immense. If the span of a genealogy is vast enough all kinds of associations appear.

The aunt who writes on the history of suffragettes enjoys the information about Constance Markiewicz.

Sometimes I dream about this aunt. In my dream we are standing in a shallow warm sea. An ocean liner is anchored close. When I wake up I find meanings for this dream, then I forget. What stays with me is a sense of stillness: my calm aunt, the sea making light of the great boat, silence.

In Aylesbury Gaol Con Markiewicz began to dream. Her sister reported that she *is always dreaming odd trifling things about me queerly correct.*

Family connections are not only in genealogies or in histories of revolutions and snipers starving at their posts; but in simple dreams, meaningful, if you like, giving a kind of direction, a navigation through the dark with closed eyes.

My child was disturbed during the night my grandmother died. I wrapped him in my arms, making a pregnancy of my arms for him. I was too uncomfortable to sleep, my thoughts were with my grandmother. Just after my grandfather's death she woke and felt his sweet weight next to her, warming her turned back. She had been alone for many years—he left her for somebody else.

We are driving, after my brother's wedding. We're driving through strange green country, blue-green, after rain, amazing pasture. If a seed falls in a road cutaway it grows. I'm in the back seat with my little boy. We live in the West, beyond the desert.

I've wasted my piebald horses on you, says my mother. Each time she sees one she thinks she can make a wish for herself, but one of us needs the wish. I don't know what she thinks I need and I don't ask.

At the wedding my cousin and I find a patch of gravel next to a weathered sandstone wall. Nobody else is in sight. He's brought me a thoughtful cigarette. He says *I wish you lived closer.*

In a taxi in William Street I think I see him on the footpath walking in the opposite direction. I feel the pull, against the acceleration of the car. He is the original for my husband. Some women look for their fathers: greying surgeons, drunks. Not me.

What I remember most clearly about my wedding is my breathlessness. The night before I tightened up with asthma. My mother brought me her Ventolin. I was propped up in my old bed, alone, waiting for the trough and crest of the next breath.

I knew he would come early the next morning, grinning, his suit in plastic over his shoulder. We didn't like to be apart.

In 1891 Lizzie Ashton told the Women's Suffrage League that after women got the vote *their first work must be to amend the marriage laws or, blasphemous as the words might sound, do away with them altogether.* This caused quite a stir. Without marriage, said the *Bulletin* in response, women will be *deserted,* in fact *the navigation of our harbours and rivers will be hampered by the remains of lost, deserted women.* It hasn't quite worked out like that. One of my friends bought her pregnancy at a clinic, straw by bright glass straw of a liquid which could almost have come from a pleasant tree.

My grandmother had a harsh marriage.

Among her things we found a watch and a leather suitcase with her initials imprinted in gold next to the handle. These were presents from her father. She was his favourite. I think of him, white-haired like a great polar bear and helpless. He gave her a gold watch and a suitcase, one standing for constancy, the other for escape. It was useless. Finally, long after her father's death, she was *deserted.*

Her watch ticks at my wrist as I write, loud with old agitation.

Yet I still did it: clipped my mother's lace veil onto my cropped boy's hair and said *I do.*

So there we are, years later, the baby and I, with a

drowsy bottle, waiting for the tender shiver of a footstep on the verandah, knowing the shiver is caused by the unsteadiness of the beams underneath the floor, knowing the very structure is unsteady.

I was warned about everything. I asked my mother what it was like to have a baby. She said, *All the points of the compass swivel*. Directions shift. I asked the hairdresser. She said, *Imagine cutting off your own leg*.

It was an unexpected pregnancy.

Here is a secret: the neat ovulation curve only exists on a chart. Babies are conceived during bleeding, in the very early and late stages of the cycle, in a last flourishing release after menopause, like Sarah in the Bible. Sensible cultures think they come as spirits in the wind.

I was friendly with a priest who was interested in books; he was a chaplain at my husband's old school. It used to be the kind of school where boys are thrown onto prefects' fists and made to dive into crowds of stinging jellyfish in the river. Ideas change. Now cartoonists and great novelists take up residencies at the school and talk to the boys about emotion and theology.

I went to a choral service in the chapel. The walls facing the river are largely glass and at this point the water looks like one of Nolan's rivers: blurs of silver and brown.

I sang until I was light-headed from lack of air, or

ordinary happiness. The woman next to me told me about her children as the offertory plate was passed. She knew that I was pregnant, although I didn't. Sometimes other women can read pregnancy in the eyes or in the slight fullness of the skin. She made a passing comment which I didn't believe or listen to. A little girl in a striped dress on the seat near us scratched between her legs for the whole service. I was only conscious of the river and the music and the bold enjoyment of the striped child.

The pregnancy was confirmed with a chemist shop test. It was in December, a few weeks before the Gulf War.

I started to vomit. I vomited so hard that my nose bled. Then I began to lose whole blood. I stood in red pools. I was getting rid of all my colour. Soon I would be translucent, like glycerine, and wash away in the shower.

Before that could happen my good actress friend visited with an armload of men's shirts to wear after I got big, and instructions to lie quite still. She had a young child, and she made me believe that there would be a baby at the end of all of this.

She told me about her labour, and the birth, when her helpers held up a baby covered in white vernix. The baby's eyes were navy and her mouth was red. She was like a character from Noh drama, foreign, masked and theatrical in her actress mother's arms.

My own artform was not reassuring. Mothers often have

a strange translucency in fiction, invisible, or shining with false radiance.

I went to a Peace service at the cathedral. I was given a candle with a cardboard collar which someone had carefully cut to protect my fingers from hot wax. There were Quakers, Buddhists, Anglicans, a row of elderly Irish nuns. Everyone had a candle with a cardboard ledge.

The war began.

A friend who is a nun told me about the young men she knew in the last war. All pilots, shot and burned.

An international group of women parliamentarians had been holding talks to try to avert the war. I remember a senator, talking and talking, vehement with jetlag and failure.

Pacifism is often seen as the special property of mothers. Bertrand Russell, in Paris for a World Government Conference, found himself in the home of Schiaparelli, the couturier whose special shade of pink once brought me so much pleasure. In Schiaparelli's garden he was confronted by women who wanted his support. They were planning to organise in opposition to nuclear warfare; they felt especially qualified to do so because of women's maternal involvement in the continuity of life.

Russell was invited to support an organisation from which he was necessarily excluded: *My wife was standing on a balcony above the garden. Suddenly she heard my voice rise in anguished tones: 'But, you see, I am not a mother!'*

I hope it was not only my pregnancy which involved me in the pain of the Gulf War, so that it lost its shape as event, as narrative, and became pure anxiety. After all, it was pure anxiety for nuns and senators, too.

A concern for children, even a passion for children, can mean very little in the larger world of politics.

My father had a workman who crimped detonators with his teeth. They must have been blowing up tree stumps, working with dynamite. The workman was unusual in two ways: his carelessness with detonators and his great affection for children. When my mother took smoko out into the paddocks he reached for the baby. The night before he disappeared, dissolving into the mangrove shanties, he was drunk and confessional. He had been a Sergeant of Police in his own country. He called on what we would now term dissidents. He took them to the river, in the night. He cut a hole in the European ice. Dropped them in. They surfaced in other countries. *Black water very fast,* he said.

Right now I am teaching my little boy his ABC. He's almost four. He's bored with cutting out and colouring in. I read him stories, we make words with a plastic alphabet. We have a chart with letters and pictures. It begins with an apple, a bird and a clown.

Sometimes I wonder if it's the right thing to do, if words aren't best left alone for as long as possible.

Writing and grief are so close in Beckett: *the eye fills*

with tears. Imagination at wit's end spreads its sad wings.

We have a book called *Norah's Ark.* In it a woman farmer saves her animals from a flood by upturning their barn and building a shelter on the interior of the watertight roof. She sits on her tractor with one fist raised. Her animals lift above dark water. Norah and the animals play 'I Spy' to pass the time. W is for water. We spell out *Ark* and *Water* with our plastic lettering. We name danger and safety from above.

It is fashionable to see language as a symptom of loss, as a substitute for maternal intimacy. Julia Kristeva writes that *the sadness of young children just prior to the acquisition of language has often been observed; this is when they must renounce forever the maternal paradise in which every demand is immediately gratified.*

It's only nostalgia, part of the Beckett fantasy of inactivity: *ah to be back in the caul now with no trusts no fingers no spoilt love.* I think of Norah on the tractor with her fist in the air, shouting *Heave* as the ropes tighten and the barn flips into an ark. I think of the dissidents sealed in dark water with *no trusts no fingers no spoilt love* and very soon, no life.

At twelve weeks there is a sensation like the smooth back of a spoon pressing as it turns.

Later the sensation is more distinctive: a bubbling, a tapping.

Later still the baby is heavy and busy inside me. It feels

like a great internal limb, dislocating, then finding its way back into its socket, again and again. Something large is breaking open, then slowly closing, in silence, in a tight wet space in the dark.

In my dream I am allowed to hold the baby. A woman gives me the baby to hold all night but it must be given back before morning. I'm not to look at the face or sex. In my dream I position the baby carefully, so that I can only see the swaddled body and the crown of the head.

In the final weeks, ligaments stretch painfully. The baby is big and upright, in the wrong position. I will have to have a caesarean.

The obstetrician tells me not to worry about the pain; he says, *You can open up a pregnant woman's stomach and find the uterus all inflamed.* It's a reaction against the hormones. He means to comfort me, to let me know that although I am in pain, the baby is not in danger. I am thinking about *opening up a pregnant woman's stomach.*

I don't go to ante-natal classes. I don't want all their information.

On the way to the clinic I listen to Elgar and Prokofiev on the car radio. *As a child*, says the announcer, *Prokofiev loved fairy tales.* He retells the Cinderella story. The Prince is looking for his bride. The pigeons say *the true bride rides with you.* He has been looking and looking, without understanding that he carried the answer to his enigma with him.

I dream that it is my wedding morning. We are to be married once more, we sit side by side for the photographer.

At the birth we hold hands very hard, our hands are white.

I feel the cutting; they say I'll feel pressure, then *pressure coming up.* The baby is pulled from within me, gasping and crying, flinging his fists up in the startled reflex familiar from the victim of the firing squad in Goya's *Third of May.* I glimpse his face before he's wrapped and given to his father.

I'm wheeled into a recovery room, I start to shake. It's the morphine. I'm shaking and shaking. They give me more oxygen. I'm taken to the ward, I melt crushed ice in my mouth and vomit.

The baby deteriorates quickly over the next few days. He is yellow, listless, baggy-skinned. He keeps losing weight. He looks at me with slightly yellowish eyes. When I speak to him in his wire crib he sucks his dummy or the back of his hand; for him, my voice means *suck.* He stares at me, sucking hard on the piece of plastic, or the flesh of his own hand. There is a sign on the end of his crib instructing me not to pick him up because holding babies is supposed to inhibit their growth. I'm on the far end of the ward. Nobody sees me sneak him into my arms.

For much of the time there is no one to notice. All the nurses are studying, hoping for management positions. One introduces herself to me. She's a Scot. *Edinburgh,* I think, *centre of medical excellence*. She tells me she's from Glasgow.

The ward is suddenly full. One of the other women had a long labour, her baby's collarbones were broken during birth. This baby cries and cries. A woman from Vietnam looks out the window. If she is offered anything, painkillers, a binder for her breasts, she refuses. *Oh doesn't matter*, she says. *One or two days sore*. When the staff ask her what she would like to be called she says, *Whatever is easiest for you*.

There is a printed list above each of us in a metal holder: Name, Consultant, Registrar, Resident, Nurse. All blank.

The babies have name-tags at ankle and wrist. The woman opposite calls her baby Adora, like the biscuit: splintery wafer and sweet cream. Or else it is a theological name, a name suggesting rapture, impossible to ignore.

The Scottish nurse pushes my baby's head around and grips my breast. I'm feeling fifteen, stuck on a piece of equipment in the gymnasium, unable to complete a manoeuvre.

We are failing to thrive.

We don't thrive until we are allowed home and I am tucked into our old high wooden bed, the baby in the curve of my arm. There is music; I missed music in the hospital. My husband brings me a plate of fish and salad: strong bright flavours. In the night the baby and I turn about each other like the planets as we shift from one breast to the other.

He does the things all other healthy babies do.

He laughs, he takes the breast in determined hands. I turn back to him in the car at traffic lights and he bursts out laughing. I give him a jelly snake and he examines it intelligently and mouths it in sections.

The house we lived in then had blackbutt floors, which sound dull, but are in fact golden, more than gold, incandescent. We spent our days on these brilliant floors.

He was *spoilt*, he should have been given *boiled water*. A baby should be *trained from the moment he is born*.

I was listening to Nabokov's *Invitation to a Beheading* on the radio. What is most chilling about the ending is the firm soothingness of the executioner, his tone of parental authority.

We are tucked into a high wooden bed. There are plates of food on the sheets, full sharp flavours, wet with green oil. There is music like a coverlet of warm air. My baby is on my lap, he has lost his hair, he has a bare Buddhist holiness. The expression on his face matches his father's, exactly. His father is at the end of the bed, leaning back against the slats.

I have never written about love, this is new to me. My characters are quite alone, at the end of every book. *Why?* I ask. It isn't a conscious wish. I don't want solitude, myself. *Solitude is a cliché of first-person narration*, he says. He's right. It's a matter of form, not something I learned in my life, in this bed, but something I learned from Beckett.

When I write about my child I cannot write about him, alone.

In the mortuary my grandmother's head faced the door, as if she heard the sound of the opening door and turned in welcome.

My mother intended to say goodbye, but she could not move.

My father stepped into the room and kissed the hard forehead ·and said, *It's just the body of your mother.* Her eyes were pointing in different directions.

I want to write about my child, but I do not want to be a pathologist in my writing, separating, classifying, under plain light.

I think of my child wrapped in a warm confusion of tissue, his own and the tissue of others, wrapped up as we all are, always, pulling away and trying to be held, seeming to turn to each other, even in dreams and in death.

References:

Samuel Beckett, *Proust*, New York, Grove Press, 1957, p 38; 'Ill Seen Ill Said', *The New Yorker*, Oct 5, 1981, pp 48–56; 'Sanies I' in *Collected Poems*, London, John Calder, 1977, p 17.

Ann and Reg Cartwright, *Norah's Ark*, London, Random House, 1983.

Anne Haverty, *Constance Markiewicz, An Independent Life*, London, Pandora, 1988, p 171.

Julia Kristeva, *In the Beginning was Love, Psychoanalysis and Faith*, New York, Columbia University Press, 1987, pp 40–41.

Audrey Oldfield, *Woman Suffrage in Australia*, Cambridge, Cambridge University Press, 1992, pp 84–85.

Bertrand Russell, *The Autobiography of Bertrand Russell*, London, George Allen & Unwin, 1967; 1872–1914, p 147; 1944–1967, p 79.

FIONA PLACE
Apocalypse Now

In many ways the story of my giving birth begins with my grandmother. And a memory of her recalling when she gave birth in a small country town. It was fast, bloody and painful. Not that she recalled it as such. She merely said the midwife came quickly and she gave birth to a boy. It was my mother who filled me in on the details. My mother who told me it was touch and go on the kitchen floor. My grandmother never mentioned any fear. Or pain. She was the same each time she broke her hip. She seemed to trust that others would know she was in excruciating pain and act accordingly. And when they were a bit slow off the mark she would pull them up in a way that would not only guarantee action, but also endear her to them.

My mother had her face slapped. 'Shut up, you stupid

bitch,' the midwife told her, pushing the gas mask back down over her mouth. She came around later to apologise— the cylinder, she'd discovered, had been empty. My mother nearly died during each of her pregnancies. But this, like so many details, I only found out by accident. I was dumbfounded. 'Why haven't you told me?' I asked her. 'I never considered it that important,' she replied. During the second, she told me, she tore right through. She was so fast she ended up on all fours, giving birth at home alone while my father stood in the street waiting to wave down the ambulance.

I do not know what she would make of my birth story. I wish I could ask her again about hers, but she died before Daniel was conceived. There was time, though, to tell my grandmother—to witness the surprise and happiness in her eyes. I was to become a mother as they had become mothers. And as I cried with her, cried for the unexpected loss of her daughter, she wept with me for the joy of the child that was to come.

I sat next to my grandmother in the nursing home as I had my mother in the hospital. In death the two women took on an even more striking resemblance: their faces almost indistinguishable. I held my grandmother's hand. She'd outlived both her children; her son dying while still a boy—a soldier in the war. Now she could join them. And with the afternoon sun fading, and only the distant sounds of the birds to disturb us, I farewelled her.

Darkness was approaching. I packed the few belongings I wanted to keep and thanked the staff. Minutes later, battling with the traffic, I was overcome by an enormous sense of responsibility—with both women gone it was I, the daughter, who must keep alive the strength and beauty of their spirits. I accelerated out of the corner and down onto the freeway, the seatbelt hugging my bulging midriff; being a mother, I realised, was now up to me.

We sit in the hospital foyer, waiting for the 'booking tour'. The automatic glass doors open and close: floral deliveries, partners, the relatives and friends of partners, swish back and forth. 'It all comes back so quickly,' I tell Tom. 'And to think in my day when I was a student nurse, we had to live in!' I also realise how at ease I will feel if the midwives have finally discarded their uniforms. 'This is excruciatingly boring,' Tom groans as our sitting extends into its second half hour. 'Let's go out for dinner afterwards,' I suggest. 'A treat.'

Eventually we, and the one other couple waiting, are met by Vaia, our tour guide. Vaia is in uniform, and instantly, rightly or wrongly, I am both disappointed and on guard. Vaia takes us up to the third floor and we follow her down the long corridor. The smells, the sound of footsteps, and the constant murmur of voices are so familiar. Vaia points to a small screen, 'When you arrive and it's out-of-hours, we can see you on the video monitor and have someone come down and let you in.'

We squash into the tiny, but brightly lit room. Vaia proudly pats each piece of equipment as she tells us what we can expect. 'Everything is here,' she reassures us, her palm resting on the resuscitation trolley. 'And when baby is born the baby doctor will come round to make sure everything is all right.'

The Greek couple smile and squeeze hands.

'You don't have to worry about a thing,' Vaia says, smiling back at them, 'we'll look after you. Now, are there any questions?'

Silence fills the room.

'Can I give birth on the floor?' I ask nervously, before the moment vanishes.

Vaia looks around the tiny room. We all then look around the tiny room.

'We have a wonderful bed,' she replies, walking over to demonstrate. 'See—it goes up, it goes down, it even bends!'

'Yes,' I nod. 'But can I give birth on the floor? Are there any beanbags?' Vaia looks puzzled. 'It is a very small room. In an emergency beanbags would be a problem.'

'Well, without beanbags then, could I give birth on the floor?'

Vaia searches the floor as though searching for clues. Why anyone would choose to give birth on the floor is obviously beyond her. Even I am surprised how much it matters. But for some reason I need to know I can be on the floor.

'No, I don't think it would be possible,' she finally replies. 'Anyway, I don't think doctor would allow it. But if you really want,' she offers, 'you could be on all fours on the bed.'

I know Judy, my obstetrician, has no problems with my being on the floor. And since Judy delivers at the hospital, I know it is possible. But I cannot imagine giving birth in a place where they refer to paediatricians as *baby doctors*. 'That truly is beyond me,' I tell Tom as we walk back out. And suddenly I am aware how much the *where* will matter—and for some reason this upsets me. I try to tell myself it is the cell-like rooms with their lack of partner rooming-in space that has upset me. But I know what I really fear is being told what to do by strangers with whom I have nothing in common. 'What if I hate the birth centre, too?' I ask Tom. 'What if it's too New Age? I don't know what I'll do.'

'At least we know one option, sterile though it may be,' Tom replies. 'But I have to say I'm a bit underwhelmed.'

'Let's go home.'

'What about dinner? Your treat?'

'I'm too depressed.'

In my ideal birth I am the sort of woman midwives dream about—*robust, sensible and gutsy*.

But I'm a wimp when it comes to pain. I'm not at all like my grandmother.

Yet I still want to give birth *naturally*. I want to believe that we can have a feel-good birth anywhere, that it will not completely rest on our choice of the *where*; that whether we find ourselves in a labour ward or birth centre, either public or private, it won't make that much difference. I have, after all, worked within the system. I am not blind, I do know the pitfalls. In fact my biggest *where* fear is that once in the *where* I will be swamped by the dogmatism of the *where*: either medical or anti-medical. I also imagine myself swanning home straight after the ideal birth with my only discomfort the wearing of a pad for a few weeks or so!

'Now, don't be too full-on,' I warn, half-joking, half-serious, as we walk towards the entrance of the birth centre, 'they're not too big on men here.'

'Okay, Helen, you're the boss,' Tom grins.

The flyscreen door rattles—it is a comforting rattle and as a non-uniformed Julie welcomes us in, I feel we may well be in the vicinity of an acceptable *where*. She takes us through to the lounge and then disappears. 'The low-key approach,' I whisper to Tom. 'We are meant to have confidence she will return.'

We sit down. The lounge room has a TV, magazines, and faded cardboard notices displaying *house rules*. There are also plenty of toys. 'Feels comfortable, doesn't it?' Tom says. I nod.

'So you think the birth centre is the place for you?' Julie asks on her return, her question directed to me.

'Yes,' I reply. 'We went to the private hospital and it was way too medicalised for our liking.'

Julie looks at me and nods understandingly.

'Way too medicalised, wasn't it Tom?' I ask, indicating to Julie that I want him included.

'Mm, definitely,' Tom agrees.

I want Julie to like us, especially me. I already know having my own obstetrician will be an impediment, that it will be read as not having faith in the midwives available at the birth centre.

'Well, if you do choose to come here you will be seen by one of the midwives each visit. And hopefully you'll meet most of us so that on the day you'll know the midwife. And as you may already know, we have a philosophy of self-care—you're expected to check your own urine and your own weight each visit.'

I nod my head, hoping Julie will also point out the toilet and weigh machine. She doesn't. Instead she takes us through to one of the rooms. There is a low-lying pine double bed, chest of drawers and ensuite. It isn't that much different to home.

'It's perfect,' I tell Julie.

Julie pulls open drawers and swings back curtains to show us how cleverly they have hidden the equipment. She then tells us they have a drug-free approach to birth, that they encourage women to help themselves, to make use of the spa, shower, hot towels and massage. 'We don't encourage pethidine or gas, we don't even have pethidine on the premises, we'd have to go up to the ward for that,' she says, leaving us alone to admire the facilities.

'What she means is if only one person is on duty, forget the pethidine,' I whisper to Tom. He smiles.

'Listen, I really want to come here, but you'll have to promise to come with me for the visits.'

'Of course I'll come, this is a joint venture, remember?'

'But what if your coming with me means the women think I'm a wimp? What then?'

'Helen, you worry too much,' he says, rolling his eyes.

'At least here we'll be together,' I smile. 'I love the idea of you being here with me, during and after the birth, and our own ensuite in which to luxuriate.'

Tom finds a small fridge. 'For the champagne,' he grins.

'I'd really like to come here,' I tell Julie.

'Fine, well I'll book you in. You're public then?'

'Um, no, I'm seeing an obstetrician.'

'Oh, I see,' Julie's voice cools dramatically. 'You are aware then, I take it, that most obstetricians aren't prepared to come here?'

'Yes, I've Judy, Judy Cramer,' I reply.

'Oh, right, Judy. Yes, she's on our list,' her voice still cool. 'Well, there's no point making an appointment for you. Shared care doesn't begin until closer to the birth.'

I hate disappointing Julie.

'Why couldn't she have found the generosity to ask why I'm seeing Judy?' I ask Tom as we drive home. 'Why can't she acknowledge my decision has more to do with the current system than anything against her personally? It's not that I don't have faith in them, it's simply that I believe you need to build a relationship in order to have faith.'

'You're right, it's not too much to expect,' Tom replies. 'And stop worrying. They'll still like you.'

In an ideal world I'd arrive at the birth centre with a midwife who knows me—with a woman I'd have seen throughout the pregnancy and who would have already spent the beginning stages of labour with me. A woman who'd only call on her team-mate, the obstetrician, if necessary. But it is not an ideal world. Private midwives usually only deliver at home, and obstetricians usually work in institutions, where they are trained for emergencies rather than to provide any emotional support during an ordinary birth. Neither option really suits me.

I need a relationship.

And this desire has led me to Judy: an imperfect choice in an imperfect world. In an emergency I want a relationship with the person who plunges into me. I want to make decisions with someone who knows me. Not that Judy is my ideal health-care practitioner. She is as grey as they come. But she is one of the few obstetricians on their list, she is accessible by public transport, and more importantly, as the visits begin to multiply, I trust her clinically.

The birth classes are held in the local primary school. Most of the couples are in their thirties and seem to take comfort in the seventies seating arrangements; the large lumpy cushions and foam-filled beanbags. Each week we do exercises and listen to stories. In my loose T-shirts and brown sandals I fit in well, but it is Tom in his more formal workclothes who is more at ease. Especially so the night we are told to groan and moan; to fake childbirth.

Swayin' an' a-rockin', all the couples in the room are going for it, but for some reason I am extremely embarrassed. 'Come on, Helen, g-r-o-a-n,' Tom encourages. I listen to him and the other couples groaning. I am taken aback by how good he is: so relaxed, so uninhibited. He is obviously enjoying himself. But as I rock back and forth with him I am too overcome by shyness to utter a single sound. He holds me gently. And teases me just enough so I don't feel *too* embarrassed.

After the exercises there are the stories. And with the lights turned down low, week after week, we are enthralled and at times, horrified. The first story we hear is from Skye and Warren, who tell us the story of their daughter Kitty's birth.

They tell us about the candles, the incense, and how they made a tiny mistake in not allowing the midwife to check on them.

Skye gave birth in the spa. The midwife told them the amount of blood floating around seemed normal. They then asked to be left alone. And the midwife left them alone. An hour later Skye was fitting. Minutes later she was fighting for her life in intensive care.

'The registrar would have freaked at the candles,' I tell Tom as we drive home. 'The staff at the birth centre would be in deep shit over that one. They should never have left her alone. They probably shouldn't have allowed her to stay in the bath.'

'It certainly didn't sound like good management,' Tom says.

'It wasn't. And if there's one thing I don't want, it's a post-partum haemorrhage.'

'You're telling me!' Tom exclaims.

While on the toilet, I note the bath needs a good scrub and that there are a couple of light brown spots on my underpants. I am intrigued. 'What do you reckon?' I ask Tom who is busy installing our newly purchased dryer. 'You think it could be *the show?*'

'Maybe, but why don't you give Judy a ring?'

'I have very small grumblings too,' I add.

'It's time to ring her then!'

I ring Judy and she says it could be either pre-labour or it may be the real thing—that I'll just have to wait and see. So I flick on the TV. And as 'The Young and the Restless' rolls through another episode, the grumblings grow from grumblings to very irregular small growls.

During the ads I pore over my pregnancy and birth manuals. I am not due for another ten days. Is this *false* or *pre-labour*? I go over and over each section. And in between deliberations on how and where we should put the dryer, Tom and I interpret and reinterpret my signs and the book's signs.

We cast our minds back through all the birth stories we have heard in the class, trying to recall if any of my signs match any of those in the stories we have heard.

Eventually we decide to do as Judy has advised—to wait and see.

I also begin to think *maybe this is it*—and am so pleased we have finally organised *baby corner*, resplendent with the Huggies, borrowed crib and assorted babywear. I feel guilty about the Huggies, but I cannot come at booking the nappy service until I have the baby. 'Just as well we've booked to have the car seat installed tomorrow!' I call out to Tom. He agrees and asks me to come and see if where he plans to fit the dryer meets with my approval. 'Hey, that's great,' I tell him, impressed with his suggestion which will still allow room for the ironing board and assorted cleaning accessories.

Having successfully inserted the dryer onto its wall brackets, Tom then decides it is time to pack an *overnight birth centre* bag. I love the idea of *him* packing the bag— it is so romantic. But I am unable to keep quiet. 'Make sure we have the Poppers, the champagne, the lavender massage oil and your swimmers,' I yell from the lounge, 'I really want you to be in the bath with me.'

I am so excited at the prospect of us being in the bath

together. Our bath at home isn't all that big and to be able to splash around in the spa at the birth centre will be so much fun. But I keep such excitement under wraps. I am still undecided, still unsure as to whether it is *false* or *true* labour.

Having ticked off everything on the list provided by the birth centre Tom lifts up my lounge-legs and sits down. 'So how are the contractions?' he asks, his hand caressing my leg.

'They're hardly anything,' I tell him. 'And I want you to go to work, I'll be fine. You're on the phone and I promise I'll ring if anything happens.'

Tom looks at me carefully. He is more than happy to stay home.

But I want the opportunity to be like my grandmother. To be cool with a capital C. I also want to experience the exhilaration, the excitement of a possible impending birth alone.

'Go!' I tell him, pushing him out the door. 'Heavens, it's only for a couple of hours, you'll be back by seven.'

I ring and leave a message for Rosie: *maybe I am in labour and maybe she would like to come over for dinner*. I then switch on the video and insert *Apocalypse Now* which I have borrowed from the local library. Having recently seen *Hearts of Darkness*, the documentary about the making of *Apocalypse Now*, I am keen to watch it again. *This is the end, this is the end, my friend*, Jim Morrison sings. There are palm trees, smoke and fire. The sound of The Doors fills the living room, the sound of choppers fills the living room. And Martin Sheen's upside-down face appears on the screen. He's waiting for a mission. And while he's waiting he loses it, his drunk hand smashing the glass mirror. He's all over the place.

Finally he collapses onto the floor. And sitting against the bed, smears his face with his blood. And screams. Only you can't hear him screaming, you can only hear The Doors. You only hear him scream when they cut the song, when he's forced under a cold shower by the soldiers who come to collect him for his mission. There is no escaping the terror ... and it is not long before my *small growls* step up a notch to *not-so-small growls*, creating a certain level of bodily discomfort which makes movie-watching alone beyond me. And pressing the stop button, I ring my sister Brenda in Brisbane.

We talk for over an hour. And Brenda is smart enough to let me chat on and on about her up-and-coming trip to Berlin, rather than my impending birth.

The moment Tom opens the door at 7.15 my *not-so-small growls* suddenly lock into gear. 'It's as if my body knows you are home,' I tell him.

'You haven't timed them until now?' he asks, surprised.

'No, not yet.'

He quickly changes out of his suit and into jeans.

Suitable *going-to-the-birth-centre attire*. Within minutes of his arriving Rosie appears. She is in her after-gym apparel. A sunflower yellow mini wrapped around a tight lycra bodysuit and Nikes.

'Hell Rosie, you sure know how to make a woman on the verge of post-pregnancy flab feel on edge,' I tease.

'Oh darling, five hundred sit-ups a day and you'll be just fine,' she laughs. 'Now, give me that book.'

She asks me question after question. And together we try to work out where I am in the labour process. 'They're not too bad,' I tell her, 'they're regular and ten minutes apart.'

'But you can still talk through them,' she replies, finally putting down the book, 'so you've probably got hours to go.'

'So what shall we do about dinner?' I ask. 'Anyone for Thai?'

'You want Thai?' Rosie asks incredulously.

'Yeah, I'm starving and there's nothing in the fridge that takes my fancy. Tom can go get it for us,' I purr in his direction.

'You want me to go out and get Thai?'

'Yeah, red chicken curry. And you and Rosie can have a drink. But not too much, I want you in reasonable shape when it happens.'

Rosie and Tom both laugh.

'Can you believe it?' Rosie turns and asks Tom. 'The woman is about to give birth and she wants Thai!'

'Look, it probably won't happen until tomorrow,' I tell them. 'And if there's anything I learned from those birth classes it was not to put too much energy into the first stage.'

Rosie looks towards Tom for guidance. 'She's right on that one, I can vouch for her on that,' he says, knowing I want him to back me up, but when necessary, be swayed by Rosie.

'Oh, come on, let's have Thai!' I tell them. 'Think of it! Yummy spring rolls, red chicken curry ... come on!' Eventually, I convince Rosie to let Tom go out for Thai. And Tom to go out for Thai. And while he is gone I debate with her whether or not I should ring the birth centre. And how we will cope with the long night ahead. 'I want to stay at home as long as possible,' I tell her.

The food tastes strange. The chilli is hotter than usual and the chicken less chickeny than usual. It's not quite as yummy as I'd hoped.

I stop eating every now and then. And with each growl I inform Rosie and Tom of the *feel*. 'It's like really bad period pain,' I tell them. 'If this is what birth is about, I don't know what all the fuss is.'

'We should ring the birth centre,' Tom says.

'Well, you ring them,' I tell him. 'I don't want to appear anxious.'

Tom phones. But Kerry insists on speaking to me.

'Hi,' I say, trying to be as cool as possible. Kerry asks

me about the contractions and as I begin talking one starts. She listens as I try to talk through it. It is becoming increasingly difficult. 'Come up whenever you want,' she tells me. 'It's up to you. I'll be here until nine and then Deirdre is on. Have you met Deirdre?'

'No,' I reply.

'Well, don't worry, Deirdre is great.'

'So what did she say?' Tom asks.

'She says come up when I want.'

'Fat lot of help that is,' Rosie scoffs.

Tom are Rosie are happy to leave for the birth centre whenever I want. I tell them I'm not ready, not yet anyway. And push the play button on *Apocalypse Now*.

Men are diving for cover, bombs are falling everywhere, but Robert Duvall, the commander, rips off his shirt and struts around with his chest bare, barking orders to his men. In the midst of such heavy shelling, it is the sign of a true psychopath. 'Can you smell that?' he asks one of his soldiers. The young boy is obviously scared shitless. 'Napalm, son. Nothing else in the world smells like that.'

The three of us discuss the utter brilliance of the scene and the total madness of the naked chest. We also discuss the looming terror—Kurtz. But as much as I want to watch Martin head up the river to confront Kurtz, to what he calls the 'worst place in the world', I lose the ability to tough it out.

The shower wins.

I cannot go through any more growls without assistance. They are too big. I want heat. And lots of it.

Rosie and Tom follow me. The growls are now five minutes apart, becoming stronger each time. 'But they are still bearable,' I tell them. 'Just.'

Minutes later I can hear Rosie and Tom conferring outside the bathroom. I know they are organising to leave for the birth centre. This pleases me enormously, allowing me to listen to my body. 'If I were going to lose it, it would be now,' I tell Rosie as she returns to the bath's edge. 'Let's go.'

Rosie nods and somehow I manage to wipe myself dry and dress.

I want to help make sure we have everything, but it takes every ounce of my mental energy to put one foot in front of the other. Things are beginning to speed up. Really speed up. And as I climb into the back of the car the growls are biting ferociously, two minutes apart.

Tom turns the key. He turns it again and again, but the car refuses to start. It's like in the movies.

'Okay, now everyone keep calm,' I order. I then scream out in pain at the top of my voice.

Finally the car starts. 'Get me to the fuckin' hospital as fuckin' fast as you can!' I scream. I scream and I scream—all the way.

I undress at lightning pace and crouch on all fours.

'The bath is running. Do you want me to examine you?' Deirdre asks.

'No,' I reply glancing upwards, 'I dread you telling me to go home.' I also cannot bear the idea of her touching me. I cannot bear anyone or anything touching my skin. A massage would be torture.

Without any warning I am blown apart. A white-hot intensity ripping through me. I am terrified. What is happening? I crawl towards the shower, leaving a spot of blood in my trail. 'That's a good sign,' Deirdre says, leaving us to it.

We have been in the birth centre all of two minutes and it is as though I am erupting. As though Mount Vesuvius resides inside me. What the fuck is going on?

I am completely overwhelmed. Overwhelmed by fear and bewilderment. No one ever warned me it would be like this. No one. No one ever told me to expect such fury. In the slightest fragment of a second I pass from thinking someone can change things to realising there is nothing anyone can do. There are no longer any choices. I am locked in. Already I sense being galaxies behind. And as though it will be a long scramble to catch up.

'Put your swimmers on,' I scream out to Tom, 'I want you naked.'

Rosie takes charge of the shower. And I yell to her the precise moment I want heat on my back and the precise moment I don't. For some reason, I cannot tolerate an ounce of hot water during the now thirty seconds between eruptions.

I do not understand what is happening. Everything is way too fast. I am exploding out of control. The pain is unbearable. And while Tom and Rosie are working so hard to be with me, I am not with them. I am too taken aback by the eruptions thundering through me—too fixated with trying to find the right scream.

It is as though if I scream right, I will feel right.

But I cannot find any scream that matches the pain.

'There's something between my fuckin' legs,' I yell.

I place my hand between my legs, it feels like a bluebottle. Maybe, I think to myself, maybe it's a cancerous growth. Whatever it is, I don't like it.

Rosie leaves the room to find the midwife.

And during a moment of pain-free silence I catch her voice, 'My friend says there's something between her legs.'

I reach out to squeeze Tom's testicles. I want to feel something squishy. But just as my hand is within reach, he wriggles out of the way. I am mortally offended. I cannot understand why he has refused me. But before I can protest I am overtaken by another furious frenzy.

Rosie returns mid-frenzy with Deirdre, who speaks briefly to Tom and then leaves again.

'You're going to be a mother in a matter of minutes,' Tom tells me.

This is the first time anything makes sense.

Tom tries to set up some sort of ritual; talking me down

during the now twenty seconds between eruptions.

'I can't! I can't! I can't!' I yell. 'I want my mother! I want my mother!'

'Do you want me to contact her?' asks Deirdre who has returned and is inching her way along the shower wall.

'No, she's dead,' I reply. Then realising I may have been a little blunt, add, 'But don't worry, it's fine,' before screeching out yet again.

'I'm going to get you to slow down in a couple of contractions,' I hear Deirdre say as she squashes down behind me.

It is too late. I feel an intense searing. And there is a baby's cry.

I hear the cry, but I do not really understand what it means until Deirdre passes a tiny blood-covered baby through my legs and into Tom's hands.

Tom holds the baby. And then slowly turning the baby over, allows me to discover I have given birth to a boy. I am speechless. It has all been too fast. I'm not ready. I then watch as he places the clamp and cuts the cord.

I cannot even imagine touching the baby. I am stuck. Paralysed. And all attempts to move me fail.

I know I have given birth, but I am still catching up. I cannot believe what has happened in the space of twenty minutes. And it takes me a while to understand what is wanted of me—to crawl over to the surgical mat in front of the bed.

As I am crawling I hear Judy arrive. I had completely forgotten about her. She smiles and congratulates me. 'You were way too quick for me!'

She is then on the floor next to me, examining the area in question and talking to Deirdre about the placenta. After some discussion a tug is made, and then another tug—and pop, it oozes out. I am amazed how juicy it looks. Judy and Deirdre then ask me to climb up onto the bed. 'You need some stitches,' Judy says. 'Deirdre tells me the baby had his arm up over his head.'

I am too scared to ask her how bad the tear is. I am also, at this moment in time, more concerned by the size of the needle she has pulled out. It is over a mile long.

'Don't you have any spray?' I ask, holding my knees close together. 'Like the footballers?'

Judy looks puzzled. I realise she has probably never even watched the Rugby League. 'What say you give me just a few minutes then?' My legs still firmly closed.

Judy shakes her head. 'Helen, it'll hurt even more if we leave you.'

'What say just two seconds then?' I ask, hoping my two-finger salute will seal the deal. Judy looks forlornly at my two fingers, but does not relent.

'Helen, I promise, it won't hurt that much.'

Slowly and reluctantly I part my legs. And as Judy plunges the needle in Tom offers me some gas. Where the fuck's that been all this time, I wonder. It is vaguely useful. I watch Judy pull and pull. 'The stitches are dissolving stitches,' she tells me. Judy is fast and in all honesty the pulling doesn't hurt that much—it is more that I simply cannot take any more action of any sort.

'How many stitches?' I ask, turning towards Tom.

'Not too many,' he replies.

'How many?'

'Twelve,' says Judy, finishing. 'And don't worry Helen, it will heal in no time.'

I want to know if I have torn right through, but I cannot bring myself to ask either Deirdre or Judy.

'Well, how bad is it? Did I tear right through like mum?' I ask Tom as the door closes behind them.

'No.'

'How close then?'

'Not that close?'

'*How* close?'

'About a centimetre, but from what I could see of it Judy did a really neat job.'

'I feel so yucky down there,' I tell them, pointing downwards. 'I never ever want to open my legs again.'

'I think you were fantastic,' Tom tells me.

'So do I,' says Rosie. 'And no thanks to that midwife, she shouldn't have left us alone, she should've told us what was happening. I never knew things could happen that quickly.'

Rosie then takes some snaps of me, of me and the baby, and of me, Tom and the baby. And Tom takes some of her and the baby. We joke about my trying to squeeze

Tom's private parts, with neither Tom nor Rosie believing that I didn't know it would hurt. 'I was upset when he moved away,' I tell them, 'I just wanted to feel something squishy.'

'Sure thing,' Rosie says.

We also laugh about the missed bath, the unused massage oil and the undrunk Poppers. And decide to put the champagne on hold. 'I could never have done it without you,' I tell Rosie. 'I can't even imagine you not being here, thank you so much.' Rosie smiles.

'I wouldn't have missed it for the world,' she says, and kissing the baby one more time, bids us goodnight.

Tom brings our son into our bed. His hands are so nimble, so gentle. And he sits gazing dreamily into his eyes.

I watch on with pleasure. I am extremely glad that one of us can pull it together. But try as I might, I cannot experience delight for myself. I am too overwhelmed, too exhausted.

'It's like getting married one thousand times in the one day, don't you reckon? I'm totally fucked.'

Tom looks at me. 'You know the wedding, how exhausted we were afterwards,' I add, sensing he is unsure as to how to take my remark.

And while desperately wishing I could focus myself solely on our beautiful son I am unable to stop questioning him. 'Why didn't any woman tell me? Why didn't they tell me it would be like a fuckin' bomb exploding? Why didn't anyone tell me the truth?'

But before he can respond, I clutch my belly and seize the moment.

'The horror,' I murmur, 'the horror.'

Post-horror, there is very little ice. They seem to treat the tear as though I am a child who's merely grazed her knee. They even have the audacity to offer me a Panadol— not even a Panadeine.

The baby, whom we name Daniel, is small for dates and the paediatrician advises against my going home early. Instead, I am transferred to a cell-like room and constantly made anxious by the knocking on my door. Uniformed midwives knock politely before proceeding to tell me I am feeding the baby wrongly. That I must listen to what they are telling me. The problem is they each tell me something different.

I can barely walk and need a rubber ring to sit. I am exquisitely elated, but bombarded with thoughts of failure: Why do I feel as though a truck has driven right through me? Why aren't I bouncing out of bed like that woman who sang a major operatic role only hours after giving birth? And why do I need to talk about the birth, over and over? I do, at least, try to tell the story humorously. And with the first part of the story, I think I succeed, with most friends laughing: 'You watched *Apocalypse Now*?' 'You ate *Thai*?' 'You didn't think it would hurt to squeeze his balls?' But I don't think I am quite so successful with the rest of the story. The entertainment level drops significantly.

I want to tell them how bad I feel. How ashamed I feel. Ashamed I didn't know how painful it would be. Ashamed about how much I need and value Tom. A real woman, I hear myself say, would manage alone. A real woman wouldn't give in to exhaustion. I, on the other hand, adore watching Tom bathe Daniel. And rely on him to attend to much of his non-breastfeeding care during the day. Judy, on her daily visits, is kind enough to advise I stay until bored.

It is, I have decided, the day to go home.

I stand in the breakfast room holding Daniel, dressed in the only decent clothes I have, when suddenly there is blood pouring down my legs. This time I know immediately what is happening. And even though I know how crucial it is to stop the bleeding, my first thought is to find someone to hold Daniel. And my second, as the drip is inserted, is whether or not I will be able to breastfeed in Acute Care. And even though I know D&Cs are as common as cockroaches, it reassures me immensely to know it is Judy who will be operating.

'Are you a birth or a miscarriage?' the theatre sister asks as she wheels me into the operating theatre. 'A birth,' I reply, stunned by her insensitivity. *Heavens woman, listen to your own brutality*, I want to scream at her, *can't you hear how that might sound to a woman who has just lost her dreams?* But I am too frightened to tick her off; too busy allaying the fear I may never see Daniel or Tom again.

The experience of giving birth is intensely personal. And every woman's experience is different. I guess I was in shock for the first few weeks. I was also acutely ashamed of my having imagined the only discomfort would be the wearing of a pad—it hurt when I sat, it hurt when I fed, it even hurt when I walked. And now when I think back to that time, a distinct memory of one of our very first family outings comes to mind. It was a wonderfully warm summer's day. Tom was pushing the stroller and I was walking very tentatively along the harbour foreshore while young girl after young girl dashed in front of me and down into the water. 'All I can think when I see those girls,' I told Tom as we sat down on our picnic blanket, 'is how innocent they are and how cruel it is they grow up to experience this!'

'Rest Helen! Rest and you will feel better,' he told me. 'Give it time—you lost a fair amount of blood.' He was right of course, but it was some time before my wound healed, my nipples adjusted, and I felt my energy return. And it wasn't until the autumn leaves began to fall that there was enough space in the birth story for the excitement of being a mother to burst through.

Today while Daniel was asleep I sorted through mum's old photos and came across some of me as a baby. I couldn't believe my eyes.

'Hey, check it out,' I told Tom handing him the black and white snapshot. 'As babies Daniel and I are almost indistinguishable!' Tom looked at Daniel and at the photo. 'Amazing! It's a shame your mum's not here to see it.'

'Yeah, I wish I could show her,' I replied.

And as I begin to compile Daniel's baby album, stopping every two seconds to remember this and remember that, to *ooh* and *ahh* about how absolutely gorgeous he was and is, I notice how the birth story has faded and Daniel has bloomed—and how every time I look at him, I am filled with joy.

The strength and beauty of my grandmother and mother's spirits, well and truly alive.

ANNETTE STEWART
'Cover Lightly, Gentle Earth'

> Here lyes to each her parents ruth,
> Mary, the daughter of their youth:
>
> . . .
>
> At six moneths end, shee parted hence
> With safetie of her innocence;
>
> . . .
>
> This grave partakes the fleshly birth:
> Which cover lightly, gentle earth.

Ben Jonson 'On My First Daughter' (1616)

I t is summer and I am five months pregnant, and lying under a tropical tree with my husband and our friend. We are near the sea. Both the men seem to have crept closer to my side as the sun rises higher, and I am aware of my swelling breasts and my belly which is like a perfect round bun. We doze in the dappled light of jungle-like leaves and trunks. I am wearing a bright green flowered bathing costume which I am finding a tight fit. Rosellas flit overhead. I have never felt more contented, more sensually aware, nor have I felt such power. It seems as if the whole world, these brilliant trees, the light and dark shadows, even the boom of the waves in the distance, have been arranged to celebrate me and my child's coming. The deepest joy I feel, though, is not this pride but the life stirring inside me, a tiny flutter like a bird's wings just starting for flight. This sensation is a new one, which I have only begun to feel in the last days. Therefore I am alarmed when the fluttering stops for brief periods, relieved when it begins again.

For I have not arrived at what seems to be this sublime moment without a lot of worry and sickness. For months I have lain flat in bed, fearing to move in case I vomited. I have eaten little apart from unripe pears, green apples and grapes. After the sickness there were the first spots of blood. 'It's nothing to worry about,' the doctor had said. 'Just waste stuff. Wait a few days then if it stops, take your holiday.' It had seemed a little strange, but everything about this first pregnancy had seemed strange. So the bleeding stopped and we have come away.

The night we arrived we moved into an unpretentious motel near the sea. It was a few miles from the nearest town, but the thought that I might be in danger had not occurred to me. It was so beautiful there. I knew I had to rest, but I was happy and drifted to and fro in a kind of trance, waiting as if listening to my little fluttering bird, while the two men drove in and out of town for supplies and a drink at the pub. There were large white breeze bricks outside our rooms. 'No need for air-conditioning here, love,' the manager said. 'The wind seems to come right off the sea.' She was right. At night and even by day the wind howled and whistled through our room. We made love time after time, meticulously but gently. As the days passed we developed a routine. In the morning we ate huge breakfasts of sausages and eggs when our friend came to our room. In the evening we did the short drive into town where we ate spicy Mexican food and watched the police discuss drug problems with the manager. The local cop was so addicted to chillies that he was, obviously, prepared to let a certain amount of grass go undetected.

Our friend left and other friends arrived with a toddler. We decided to move into the centre of town so as to be right at the sea. One day they all drove to Surfers but I decided to stay because I thought the long trip might not be safe for the baby. In any case I didn't feel lonely: I had the baby inside me for company. The baby and I went for a swim. The waves were high. We floated gently for a time, then had a long hot shower. I did worry that this might be overdoing it, but it was delightful to feel the hot water trickle over my by now huge belly and breasts. But just before the others returned I began to bleed and this time it was bright red blood. I was very frightened and no one knew what to do, so the motel manager's wife called a doctor. He came at once, a gentle sympathetic Asian, and his sad face confirmed my fears: 'My dear, you must come to the hospital at once.'

I was terrified. I hadn't been in a hospital since I was six years old. (You will notice that this narrative centres on 'I'. At this time no one except the baby and I seemed to count. I suppose that is the enormous complacency of the pregnant woman.) I don't even remember now what the others said or how their faces looked. There was the toddler Simon running in and out of our rooms, which compounded my disbelief that this was happening to me. The men I think looked puzzled and our friend even faintly annoyed. My girlfriend, mother of the bouncing rosy-cheeked Simon, was sympathetic but uncomprehending. She lent me a pink nightie to wear to the hospital, which only reduced me to further tears.

The hospital, when I'd sufficiently come to my senses to take stock of it, was what used to be termed a Cottage Hospital, a low, friendly looking fibro building, with a flower garden. Nurses flitted about briskly but the atmosphere was cosy. I began to feel safe and reassured and happy. Perhaps I wasn't in danger after all, perhaps the baby would be all right.

Days passed. I settled in and although I couldn't move

from the bed, there were visits from my husband and the doctor. I thought that perhaps if I adopted an optimistic approach everything might get better. I had no books to read, no work with me to fill in the days, so I meditated a lot. I remembered the story of Sophia Loren, who had been in the same predicament herself. After many miscarriages, she had booked into an expensive hotel, and had not budged for several months. She concentrated all her attention on having her baby alive and well and born at full term. *So will I*, I determined. It had worked for her, and she went on to have another as well.

So it continued for two weeks. My husband left for home, three hundred kilometres away, on an undisclosed mission, which I later discovered was to ask advice from my usual doctor. His departure did not trouble me much. I had the baby to think about all the time, which required all my efforts. And as it happened the town was situated near the home of some relatives, people we hadn't even looked up. I'd nicknamed the area Doone Valley on our honeymoon trip there a few years before, because I was a Catholic, and the family were staunch Methodists and we had decided to be silent if religious matters arose. This had made me feel like Lorna Doone in the territory of the Ridds. These family people, whom I hardly knew, were now extremely kind. They visited me. Cousin Flo was first to arrive, even though it was a thirty-kilometre trip over a winding mountain road, and she had to leave her farm unattended. 'Let me in!' I heard her shout to the nurses. 'She's me cousin.' On Sundays Uncle Harry came as well, bringing his precious Honda which rarely left its garage except for state occasions. He sat lugubriously, hat in hand, looking like an undertaker. He muttered darkly: 'Don't know what to make of that 'usband of yours. 'e took all the washing 'ome in a wet bundle. I told 'im it'd streak but 'e wouldn't listen.'

Another diversion was my daily bowel movement, the wonder of the staff. These were only achieved with difficulty, as I was so constipated from lying around. By dint of staring at food advertisements in the women's magazines, especially those involving eggs or oil, each day I could produce something black, which was taken away and examined with as much care and interest as would have been something similar from the bowels of Louis Quinze. I also listened to the gruesome details of the nurses' love lives, and helped the matron choose a design for her beach cottage from the magazines. I found one which I liked but she didn't, a Japanese model with sliding shutters and paper walls.

The biggest and most alarming diversion was the night when two local girls were brought in during the first stages of labour. The walls of the hospital were thin, and you could hear everything. They arrived all giggling and happy, but by two in the morning this had radically changed to screams and other sounds, especially four-letter words. The cacophony increased when their husbands, employees of the abattoir, arrived. 'Are the husbands going to watch?'

I hissed at the nurse who came in to reassure me. 'Of course,' she said, 'they're used to that sort of thing.' At this point I did wonder why I was trying so very hard to achieve what they were going through. Up till almost then I hadn't seriously thought about it. Having a baby was to me a vaguely romantic notion like the idea of getting married had seemed: something I had wanted to do for a long time, a goal. Not a horror, as these births appeared to be.

At about dawn the agonies of the night were rewarded by babies' cries: the infants, both males, had arrived safely. By next morning the two mothers were out and about, briskly discussing feeding. That'll be me in a few weeks, I thought happily. If I just lie here and don't move. Do everything I'm told. Concentrate all my thoughts.

This peaceful and deluded reverie was shattered by the news, shortly after, that I was to be moved home by air ambulance. I did not want to go. That very night, before I left, I began to feel my stomach contract, but was told this meant nothing in particular. Next morning I was taken by road to the airport, about thirty kilometres away, then loaded onto a tiny plane. I was extremely nervous, especially when I noticed from my prone position two large paint tins containing what could have been blood, although how this would have been put into me I could not work out. The ambulance drivers also loaded into the plane a grim-faced nurse, who looked nearly as apprehensive as me, and was obviously worried that I might give birth in the air; there was also another patient, moaning with appendicitis pains. The flight was long and touched down at several towns. I was frightened for my baby, especially as I couldn't feel the fluttering any more, only contractions. The plane bumped its way, rose and fell in the wind. I felt as if my little bird was being crushed in an iron cage.

When we touched down at home, I felt relieved and safe—that foolish delusion that going to a hospital means you will be all right. The doctor reassured me: 'I think it's a *placenta praevia*. If you can hold on for a few more weeks we'll give you a quick caesar.' He was angry with the hospital that had detained me: 'You could have died over there. They don't have proper facilities—not even a blood bank.' I thought of the two paint tins, and remained silent, but in my heart I wished I had been able to stay where I was. Have given birth to my child in that friendly seaside town. That night the contractions seemed to ease off, however, and I drifted peacefully off to sleep.

But that night was the night when my dreams and hopes ended. I woke suddenly at dawn to feel strange sensations in the lower part of my body. It wasn't pain, but a tiny head pushing down and through and out. My baby's head. What was it doing there, between my legs? I rang the bell and nurses rushed in, bundled me onto a stretcher and raced me to the delivery room. The baby was born minutes later. I heard a cry, a weak and very sweet sound. Just once. Then everyone was very quiet.

The midwife said, 'Your baby has been born. It's a little girl.'

'Please take her away,' I answered, 'I can't bear it.' They did so. Then the doctor came, looking very pale in the early morning light. By then I was becoming aware of the room I was in—it had awful light green walls, and the doctor was in green too. He said, 'Your baby has been born, but she's very weak and small. She only weighs one pound.' I desperately tried to imagine what a one-pound baby would look like and could only think of a pound of butter. I gave them my husband's number and he came to see the baby, but I didn't want to see her.

She died two days later. The doctor said, 'It's for the best. She never would have had a healthy life—you never would have been free from worry as long as she lived.'

I was profoundly shocked, and unable to care for anyone else. So my husband had to make the funeral arrangements. The best I could do was to arrange for the husband of a friend, a kindly and stalwart man, who had also experienced with his wife the agony of miscarriages, to accompany him to the burial. While this was going on the doctor urged me to take anti-depressants, but these made me feel worse, like I wanted to jump over the hospital balcony. So I asked to be taken off them. I never knew how my husband felt because we did not discuss our feelings, perhaps out of concern for one another at the time.

I didn't know how I was going to be able to continue

my life without my child, and little help or advice was available. One of the worst things I remember was the priest's hospital visit. He came around soon after our baby was born and said we should get her baptised quickly since she would not live long. I agreed to this. Then he asked about the name and said, 'Would Agatha do, since it was Our Lady's mother's name?' I was too weak to disagree, but hated it and later we changed the name on the birth certificate to one we both liked, Mary Catherine, and this made us feel happier. It gave us the feeling that she had existence, and she has remained in my mind as Mary ever since.

The same priest came back later to comfort me. Dinner had just been brought in, but I didn't fancy any. When he saw the tray he said, 'Gee, you're lucky. I'll have to wait another hour for mine.' He displayed no concern for what might have been our feelings of loss.

Another very bad time was when I woke up the morning after Mary Catherine had died and went out to the bathroom. On the way I noticed a whole trolleyful of beautiful pink newborn babies being wheeled along to be fed. Soon after this I asked to be sent home.

I recovered from the immediate shock of the loss after a few weeks. Crying in the morning at a regular time offered relief. I also went back to teaching in my university position at the beginning of term; and thinking of others, and the routine, were helpful. But sometimes in the months that followed I felt pangs of grief so agonising that I wanted to go into the garden and dig and dig into the ground so as to be with my child, where I felt I belonged.

In the year after Mary Catherine died I began to try to have another child. There was another miscarriage at eighteen weeks, and we began to despair of ever having a healthy baby. Finally we did, but the earlier episode had left its mark. I was in acute anxiety during this whole pregnancy and even after the much longed-for event, I was very tense and felt unwell. The loss of Mary Catherine was a large contributing factor to my depression, despite now having a successful birth. With this loss I felt at the time that I had also lost my youth. But I was only thirty-two, and much still lay ahead of us.

Years after: We have another daughter, who is the central person in our lives. She is a happy-natured and self-confident one. I know that Mary Catherine would have been different from this—I picture her as a bit shy, hard to coax along, unsure of herself, as she would have been when she started high school. She would have been clever but over-sensitive, capable of feeling pain.

There's a girl up the street I sometimes see with her mother, getting out of the car after school. They talk to each other and look happy, as if they have a close relationship. I don't know the family and have wondered why I keep looking at this girl. She is very tall and fair, a bit awkward in her movements, but elegant too. Obviously she isn't going through that unpleasant and difficult adolescent passage that some girls experience. Perhaps she will be a late developer, as Mary Catherine would have been.

There are other tales to tell, but this is Mary Catherine's one. The cry I heard at the moment of her birth is still greatly treasured. It is the only sound of hers that I shall ever hear. How can I express the love I still feel for our eldest child?

My little girl, my youngest but only child, often asks me about her dead sister: 'When are we going up to the cemetery, Mummy, to take Mary Catherine some flowers?' I say, 'One day, my love.' But we never have.

NONI HAZLEHURST
Babies and Beyond

How did they do it? The women who came before us, who had so many children. No gadgets, no mod cons, nothing. How did they find the time? 'Life was simple then.' But even so, take away the stress of modern life, just one child can fill every moment of every day. There's never nothing to do. Never a time you can sit back and say, everything's done.

The tasks never finish, the lists never end. And the cry 'Mum, Mu-um, Muu-uum . . . !' echoes so that you're never sure whether it's real or imagined.

But the love. The heartbreaking, gut-wrenching love. It can shatter anger, betrayal, sadness, sleep, in a moment. The love that spreads its warm fingers around your heart, through your body. That can strike like lightning.

Knee-weakening love. Warm but tinged with blue. A fear

within the soul, a longing for the child to come through life's demands completely unscathed. But to be alone, without a child to care for (doesn't have to be one's own), feels like it would be half a life. A life adrift, half grown. Being close to a child fills you with life.

Fuller, richer, busier, all things considered, I join the unbroken line. The mothers' club. Go through the gate, the point of no return . . . in fact it means opening so many doors, going down hundreds of corridors, no point in hanging back.

To love and be loved unconditionally is the beyond of all babies. The dream we've all dreamed. Simply, rainbow's end.

It was not my intention to contribute a kind of free-form, stream-of-consciousness 'piece' to this anthology. But when I sat down to write, that's what came, and the reason I offer for it is that having children can, from time to time, render a parent incapable of long thoughts or extended statements. John and I speak in a kind of shorthand now, trying to cram as much information as is humanly possible into the ten seconds or so usually available between interruptions from the children.

Having young children has certainly changed my life, in ways too numerous to count. 'Complicated' is the word that sums up the experience most accurately.

My brain reels from one half-formed thought to the next. Unwritten lists of things I was supposed to do, have to do, and will never do, dance like leaping leprechauns through my brain, whether I'm awake or asleep. I've heard many women—including myself—say that they need a wife; that having children and working and maintaining a home (as expected) is beyond most parents, singly or in pairs. Men tend to dismiss this idea, calling it 'sexist', still uncomfortable with the reality that domestic duties need to be shared equally.

And tucked in amongst all this busy-ness and stress is the ever-present guilt. After my second child was born, and the 'three days after' hormonal attack plunged me into the depths of depression, I mourned all the lost opportunities for my first child and I to experience things together. The bushwalks we should have gone on; the camping we didn't get around to; the drawings we didn't do.

When he was three months old, I was asked to go to Melbourne to meet an English director, to discuss a role in a mini-series. I certainly needed the work, having been 'laid up' for quite a while. But I didn't know whether I could justify dragging the baby to Melbourne and back in a day. The director offered to meet me at Melbourne airport, which was a big concession on his part. But I still didn't know what to do.

I rang the midwife who had shepherded Charlie into the world, and tormentedly asked her advice. Her response was swift: 'Being a mother means feeling guilty all the time, so you may as well start now!'

We made the trip and Charlie coped beautifully. Hugged to my bosom the entire time, he barely stirred. Naturally, I didn't get the role—I probably looked like the wreck of the Hesperus!

But the midwife was right about the guilt. We're told not to be so hard on ourselves, yet not a day passes without me feeling like an inadequate, unfair monster at least once. Every single time I walk out the door or leave my children with someone, I worry that they might suffer in some way. Every time I shout at them I feel dreadful, and if I make them cry I spend hours thinking about how I could have handled things better.

I wish I could give my children idyllic childhoods. I worry that they will look back and only remember that mum and dad were always so busy.

One thing I've learned through experience is how much children mirror the state you're in. I couldn't understand why Charlie behaved impossibly at the worst possible times, until it hit me that he was picking up on my craziness. If my brain was boiling, he'd either throw a tantrum or develop a fever.

Making that connection was a huge breakthrough. I've realised that you just can't fool children. They may not understand what's going on intellectually, but their sensory receptors and bullshit detectors are infallible.

My children, in fact all children, teach me constantly by example, how to slow down, to stop acting, simply to 'be'.

We expect so much of them, especially when they're very small. And in our strivings to help our children to be socially acceptable, we try to teach them to 'behave'. When times are hard, when they are screaming because *we* don't understand *them*, it's tempting to wish they would just grow up and understand what we're going through. Yet so many of the everyday situations that we put our children in today are unnatural and stressful.

When I was little, 'going to the shops' meant a leisurely walk in the pram to the local shops, where everyone knew us by name and greeted us warmly. We belonged. Occasionally we walked a bit further, to the bigger shops, but essentially it was a safe, calm, totally predictable experience that affirmed our place in the world and excited us, without overstimulating us to the point of hysteria.

Today's small urban child has to endure so much more—being strapped (sometimes wrestled) into a car seat, the stress of negotiating the traffic, finding a parking spot, getting through the carpark alive; only to be plonked into a metal trolley to spend hours under fluorescent lights surrounded by miserable shoppers, being bombarded by sounds, sights and stress from all directions. Then there's the interminable wait at the checkout, and back to the carpark to struggle home. The wonder is that tantrums are only occasional occurrences.

And through all this we expect small children to be pretty reasonable, to respond to comments like 'What's wrong with you?', 'Do you have to talk all the time?', 'Stop ya whingeing', 'No you can't', 'Put it back', 'Don't touch', and the all-time dopey question—'Do you want a smack?'

Most of us have little choice about where we live, and children have even less. The consequences of modern city living and its dehumanising effects are frightening, not just to contemplate, but to witness.

Our family lives in the country, a choice governed mostly by economic circumstances. Commuting to work isn't easy, but the huge advantage is that our children are growing up in a relatively free and safe environment. They can play outside in the dead-end street if they like. They have fresh air and quiet and a sense of their place in the community.

I know they can't be protected forever, but the thought of small children labelled 'difficult' who have to live in cramped city housing, or children who are fed drugs like Ritalin to keep them quiet and easy to control, makes me furious.

How do you explain to little ones why we need to be out of the house for up to twelve hours a day, why they can't run around wherever they want, and why people and places might be unsafe? And how do we make them happy about it?

The simple fact is, we can't. We can only do our best.

There's never enough time to do everything we have to do, and in a society that honours the dollar above all else, children and parents come way down the priority list.

Mothers—and fathers to a lesser extent—are constantly exhorted to take time out, to pamper themselves and not let their children rule their lives. But it's not easy to justify taking time off when you want your children to have everything you've got to give them, and when you feel that you owe them more of your time.

I could never have predicted or imagined the feelings of pure altruism and selflessness I have now. Like many people I worried that I was too selfish to have children. But I decided that it would be okay because I would be totally organised, completely prepared, that my children would be beautifully behaved and happy to work to my rules and my timetable with full cooperation.

I was thirty-four when I had my first child—that's a lot of years spent getting set in my ways. The shock when complete chaos descended in the form of a baby and his needs, was total. If John hadn't already had children I think we would probably have separated in the first months of Charlie's life. I was all over the place emotionally, but mostly towards the hysterical, depressed, worried end of the spectrum. John instead was always calm, and he always managed to calm the baby down, which made me feel even worse.

My other life, the one I used to have, is a hazy memory from the distant past. Images of sitting down reading a book, going out, playing the piano and looking at the shops, all swim to the surface occasionally, to remind me of how things used to be. Children may not fulfil you, but they definitely *fill* you.

I loved being pregnant. I wanted to be pregnant again as soon as Charlie was born. Both boys were born at home, for which I am profoundly, eternally, grateful.

The births were different. For Charlie I was very alert, bossy and well-behaved. After nearly four hours of pushing my insides opened up like an earthquake and out he came. In midsummer, a thick mist and thunder surrounded us for the ten minutes around his birth time, and hundreds of butterflies hovered at the windows.

With William I totally surrendered. I couldn't speak properly, only mumble. He was much easier to push out, and I felt much more peaceful after his birth. He's like that anyway. But knowing that I'd managed once and could again made a huge difference to how I felt; and my sense of well-being, as opposed to boggle-eyed, gob-smacked panic, was a great relief.

Only two things were clear after both births: that my body had just performed the most extraordinary miracle, and that I would never be the same again.

Each birthday has made me grieve. Especially the early

ones, when I couldn't pretend my baby was a baby any more.

My first son was breastfed until he was three years and two months old. Secretly I loved the fact that he still wanted me, but I finally succumbed to the pressure from those around me to stop. Two nights later I told him there was just enough for one more feed, and I cried while he contentedly sucked. A week after that he saw a picture of a cow with a full udder and said, 'I wish I was that cow's baby'.

My second son weaned himself at eleven months and I was heartbroken, feeling I'd let him down. I'm unable to accept that I may never experience breastfeeding again. It's too sad.

So why do I want more children?

Because I loved being pregnant and giving birth. They were the most extraordinary times of my life.

Because my boys are divine. Even at their worst, my love for them takes my breath away.

Because in those rare moments when the two of them are loving each other unconditionally my heart just about bursts.

Because to be given the gift of a child to love and take care of is simply, unbelievably wonderful and grounding.

A million reasons.

On one level, I still don't believe I'm a mother, and can't comprehend the enormity of the responsibility involved. But the fact is, I am a mother. I am responsible and if anything ever happened to hurt them I would be devastated. If anything *does* happen, I am devastated.

They will always be 'my babies', and I love them more than I can say.

RACHEL WARD
Milk Fever

I t must have been the barking that woke her. The knock was innocuous, almost merry. Tat-tat. An Avon lady making do without her ding-dong. Nothing unusual, nothing to fear. Twisting her head on the pillow, she read the hands on the bedside clock. Three o'clock. *Three o'clock?* Avon ladies don't knock on doors at three o'clock in the morning. They don't usually knock on doors two hundred kilometres deep into Arnhem Land either. A charge of electricity ran up her spine and burst like a silent firecracker between her ears, showering her body with goose bumps. Sweat glands prickled as they opened, making her want to scratch. Cath held her breath so she might catch the friendly whisper of her name, the shuffle of familiar feet, another knock, or the rattle of corrugated iron as the front door opened, but she could hear nothing beyond the inane yapping of dogs and her own thumping heart.

'Useless as batshit,' Gavin called these dogs. He had wanted to drown this last litter as he had done the time before, pulling the pups off Lady's teats when they were no more than a few days old, tossing them into a hessian sack and plunging them into the bathtub while Lady stood by, twitching her ears with incomprehension; then, when no more bubbles surfaced, trotting after Gavin and the dripping sack. For days afterwards Cath watched Lady try to make sense of their disappearance, staring into the murky bath water, now filled with soaking clothes, then trotting down the path to the incinerator. Scratching and whining at its base until her paws were raw. This last time Cath promised Gavin that she would find homes for the pups if he spared them. And she had, all but the last useless two.

Useless except to herald the presence of someone outside your door. Someone who didn't know that one quiet word or a scratch under the chin would calm them. Someone who appeared unfamiliar with outback habits, that a door is never locked, that company after weeks, even months, of isolation is always welcome. Why didn't they just turn the handle and come on in? Why, if they came to do mischief, did they knock at all? Why, if they came in peace, didn't they call out, 'Hello, anyone home?' or knock again? Should she call out? Lie still, or hide? Where? Cath's brain whirled like a poker machine. But the various clues and options wouldn't add up and no answer tumbled forth, like pennies through a chute.

Come on, knock again, please knock again, Cath whispered in the dark. Make it timid, apologetic to be calling so late, or a woman's knuckle, staccato and light. Oh please, Cath thought, let it be the merry little tat-tat of an Avon lady who's lost her way. Cath's pulse steadied for a moment as she imagined herself nipping out the back to start the generator so that they might share a pot of tea while they sampled lipsticks on the back of her hand or whispered platitudes over the beauty of her sleeping child.

But although the dogs continued at their feverish pitch, no knock came. Cath imagined them circling the house, perhaps looking for a window. The house was completely open. Corrugated flaps could be secured in the monsoon season, otherwise only flyscreens offered protection against intruders. Nothing a knife couldn't get through. Or a death adder, as one had a few months back. She had found it snuggled up beside her sleeping baby on a mattress in the living room. At the time Cath had not panicked. As Gavin was often heard to say, when challenged for leaving his young wife alone in the bush so often, 'she has more bush smarts than most abos north of Alice.' Grabbing Hughie by the singlet she had plucked him out of harm's reach. Then taking a broom had swept the drowsy adder through the door, nudging it until it slipped back into the bush. But, since that time, Cath could hardly ever be persuaded to put the child down. Although she had patched every probable hole she never felt quite sure of the adder's passage or, in fact, how several feral cats had found their way inside. So taking an old padded saddle blanket and the strap off her guitar, Cath made Hughie a papoose and forever after strapped him to her.

But it wasn't only the incident with the death adder that haunted Cath. In her early pregnancy she had worked beside Gavin for the Territory's buffalo eradication program, driving buffalo through the bush to pens where they could be slaughtered and burnt, ostensibly to stop the spread of foot-and-mouth disease. The operation had taken several months of scouring the depths of Arnhem Land for the elusive beasts until they'd gathered a herd of over two hundred head and travelled as many kilometres. Cath had witnessed several births along the way and, although she did not actually pull a trigger, she was there at the end. She watched the buffalo jostling and butting up against one another in the tight confines of the pen, their necks strained up over another's flank, their eyeballs stretched grotesquely to see behind themselves. She watched as small calves became separated from their mothers and then trampled in the fray. She watched the men load their rifles and set their sightlines, and she heard Gavin's call of 'fire' above the braying din. Once the firing began Cath had covered her eyes and if they cried out she could not hear above the noise of gunfire, but she never forgot the smell of their breath, rancid with

fear, the quiet of the aftermath and the milk dripping
from swollen udders into the dust.

Cath lived in a world where life was given and taken
so frequently and with such ease that when Hughie slipped
from between her thighs six months ago and took his first
sobbing breath, she well understood the precariousness of
it all. The ease with which he could be taken from her.
At first, recognising the huge gamble a mother takes in
loving too deeply, she tried to protect herself against
loving Hughie too much. She averted her eyes when he
gazed at her as he fed. She pulled away when his little
hand reached up to pull her nose, or tightened around
her finger. She pretended not to notice when his body
convulsed with pleasure at the sight or smell of her and
she refused to soothe him with whispered declarations of
love. But Hughie kept nudging away at her resistance,
prying the door open wider and wider right up until the
incident with the death adder, when Cath finally realised
the futility of her guard. Then taking Hughie in her arms
and showering him with all her withheld kisses and tears,
she surrendered to the terrible possibilities of loving too
deeply.

Gavin was away as he usually was at this time of year.
It was mustering season and after he had weaned, inoculated
and sent his own yearlings to market he worked on other
stations, sometimes as far away as Katherine, where he
was now, not due back till the end of the week. Cath
was usually glad of that. Gavin was impatient with her

fears. 'Oh, for Christ's sake put him down,' he'd say. 'You'll turn him queer.' On several occasions he had tried to pull the child off Cath's nipple while she slept but Cath would always wake and cling on tight. When he complained he couldn't sleep with the baby wriggling and shuffling beside him she would spend night after night draped like a guardian angel over the bassinet. 'Come to bed Cath,' he'd coax, way after midnight. 'Nothing's going to happen.'

'I know, I know,' she'd reason. 'But if I imagine the worst then maybe I'll safeguard the worst from happening.'

The dogs had quietened now. She could hear the remaining weaners, too small for the first trip to market, bleating from the cattle yards and a mother's mournful bellow, relentless, pitiful, tearing at Cath's conscience as it always did. It was Cath's job to keep up the hard feed and water to the weaners while Gavin was away. There was one in the yards she knew was dying. The mother knew too, and although most of the other cattle had been forced to return to the bush to find food, she stayed behind, waiting for it to die before moving on. Cath dared not let the weaner go. Gavin had accounted for them all. It would only substantiate his opinion that giving birth had made her soft in the head. Perhaps it had. Perhaps there never had been a knock. Perhaps it was only the scent of a wild boar that had excited the dogs. Or dingoes rummaging in the garbage. Yes, that was it, Cath convinced herself. The fact that the dogs would surely have taken off after them was not a logic that she wished to pursue.

Cath lay on her side, the baby's head propped against her upper arm so that he could suckle. She wouldn't sleep well and by morning her nipples would be picked and sore but Cath didn't care. She liked to spend the night with her face so close to the top of his head that every time she inhaled, the fine hairs would stand up and brush against her lips and his milky sweetness slip down inside her. Cath smiled at the thought of Gavin's exasperation as she recounted this latest example of her paranoia. He wouldn't laugh with her. He couldn't afford to. The burn-off season started at the end of the month. They had no money to hire an extra hand and Gavin couldn't do it alone. He had brought home tins of formula from his last trip to town and had already spoken to Daphne from the Lotus Creek reserve. She would take the child as soon as he was weaned. Cath had pushed the tins to the back of the cupboard but, before leaving for Katherine, Gavin had extracted a promise. Tomorrow, thought Cath, as she floated away on the steady waves of Hughie's breath. Tomorrow I'll start weaning.

Then the knock came again. And no Avon lady this time. Now an irate creditor, a man's knuckles, sure and irritable. Confident that there was someone home but not to him. Cath slipped instantly back into the shroud of terror that only moments before she had felt safe to discard. Why, she wondered, foolishly pulling the sheet up over her head, did he not call out? Demand that she open the door, threaten her. Do something. His lack of verbal assault didn't make sense. Maybe she should call out, 'Hold on a moment, I'll be right with you,' the innocence and sweetness of her voice deflating his aggression. But she dared not for fear of advertising her aloneness. His ignorance of that fact was the only thing Cath had in her favour. For a moment he appeared more foolish than her. Pounding away, when all he had to do was turn the handle, push through the dark and strip back a thin floral sheet.

Maybe he was scared too. He wasn't to know how helpless she was. He probably expected some resistance, some retaliation. A Crocodile Dundee type packing lethal weapons, daring the intruder in or just blasting him to buggery. 'Warfare is always psychological,' Gavin had told her once after he'd faced down a buffalo five times his size. 'The victor is always the one who convinces his opponent that he is less afraid.' She imagined Gavin in her place, snapping on lights, full of indignation and confrontational bluster. But even if the generator had been on and Cath could have switched on the lights she would not have done so. Her vulnerability demanded more cunning. Gathering Hughie up into the crook of her left arm, she flung back the sheet and stole from the bed. When he came to get her she would be ready.

It was a moonless night. As thick and black as the molasses that dripped from the barrels in the cattle yards.

Cath had to push away the blackness as she went, careful not to bump the door jamb or kick a shoe across the floor. There was a telephone somewhere. A satellite connection, as they were far too deep in the bush to be on a main line. Cath tried to remember where she had last seen it. It never rang much when Gavin was away. The jack, she knew, was somewhere to the left of her feet. Careful not to wake the baby in her arms, Cath bent down and fumbled along the wall for the outlet and, finding it, felt her way along the line. She would call the police. The extreme improbability of a police car being within a two-hundred kilometre radius was not her concern. Once she got through they would find some way. Helicopter maybe. Maybe they'd tell her to put him on the phone, reason with him, threaten him, whatever it took. Cath had now reached the end of the line. She had the little connecting gadget in her fingers but no phone. The phone had gone.

She had no time to wonder where: there was a further strike against the door. Low down this time, as if made with a boot. The corrugated iron rattled in its frame. Cath cursed the dogs for their barking, which had escalated to even further levels of excitement. She could imagine them straining against some invisible line over which they dared not step and was almost pleased to hear their shrill yelps of pain and the hollow thuds as his boot struck their stomachs. They would slink back under the house, their ears flat, their beady eyes full of hurt and cowardice, as they did whenever Gavin kicked them for fighting. She felt no pity. Only contempt for their failure to protect her. She would shoot them if she ever got another chance.

Hughie stirred in her arms. Cath rocked him urgently, poking a nipple too roughly between his lips. He spat it out and rubbed the sleep from his eyes. 'Shhhh,' Cath crooned, uselessly pressing her finger against his lips. It would only be a matter of moments now before he gave them away.

The gun, Cath knew, was above the sink in the bathroom. It was the only room that possessed an interior door, and so, to keep the dogs and flies out, had become the best room for hanging fresh meat, cleaning skins and by default, keeping a gun. Using the gun, mostly to shoot roo or wild boar to feed those useless dogs, was as much of a daily ritual for Cath as cleaning her teeth. It no longer seemed odd to her that her toothbrush should share a shelf with a shotgun or that the roo skins, sometimes left in the sink before salting, should be splattered with toothpaste. But the idea of standing in her doorway with the gun pointed at another human being, spouting lines from a bad 'Bonanza' script like 'Come one step further and I'll shoot,' was one that Cath found hard to take seriously. 'Oh, get real,' she imagined him saying, scoffing at the sight of her, naked, a baby under one arm, a gun under the other. At this point, however, she had little choice but to convince him, and herself, of her commitment to using the gun. She was a good shot. Only this evening she had taken the ute down to Kangaroo Flats and killed a large red male. She rarely needed to use a second bullet. As always, she had trussed the animal on the spot and thrown the dogs a fresh limb each.

But, Cath now remembered, the carcass had been unusually big, requiring both hands to drag it inside. The gun was still in the ute outside.

Before she could even feel the bite of her disappointment, a light blasted through the front window and fell exactly where she stood. Hughie turned and buried his head in Cath's armpit but Cath stood still, blinking like a stunned rabbit into what seemed to be the headlights of his car. Another smash against the door slapped her back to sense. Cath scurried blindly through the darkness to where Gavin hung his knife on a nail. It was a knife that Gavin prized. A knife he sharpened daily, spitting onto his block of granite, repeatedly testing for perfection on the edge of his thumb and squinting into the sun as he held it up for inspection. But of course the nail was vacant. The knife was gone too. Gone with Gavin.

The blows were relentless now, the corrugated iron beginning to puncture and buckle under his force. Hughie began to wail. Pressing him to her, Cath wrapped her arm around his head and rocked him gently, smiling down at him and singing as she did when the rains came and thunder shook the house as it shook now.

Looking back, Cath could not remember at what point

she stopped being afraid. Her obsessive vigil was over. An obsession not predicated on neurosis, paranoia or any other aspect of creeping madness but simply on a mother's instinctive knowledge that sooner or later she was going to lose her son. And now that she knew she would be going with him, the fear that had blanched her blood since Hughie was born, was gone. Cath felt a little lightheaded, a little shaky as her blood seemed to flow, for the first time in months, thick, crimson and hot. This close to death Cath had never felt so alive.

The door snapped open and rebounded a couple of times against the inside wall before settling ajar. Cath could see a thin sliver of starry sky in the blackness. Nothing else. Across the floor fell a sharp yellow light that widened as the door opened, devouring her in its sweep. The car was parked not more than two metres beyond the door. This close, the headlights produced little ripples of heat that made the dust particles jostle and warmed Cath's naked body. Closing her eyes, she imagined that she stood, as she sometimes did after a particularly cold night, warming her sore, cracked nipples in the morning sun. Cath shivered as a cloud passed over. Opening her eyes she finally saw him.

A black shape was framed in the open doorway, all detail obscured by the blast of light from behind, but one arm extended a good foot by whatever hung from it. As he began to move towards her the black indents of his legs and arms cut shafts through the yellow light so that his shadow fell ahead of him, smothering her with his looming presence. The baby, now thoroughly engaged by this unusual night-time entertainment, had stopped crying. His body, Cath could feel, was tense with excitement, his feet kicking in anticipation of the attention strangers usually paid him. They'd swing him in their arms and coo like doves if he smiled at them. He was smiling now. Cath knew without looking because his head was bobbing about unsteadily on his neck and his small brown wrists were flapping in delight.

Cath inched backwards as the intruder advanced. Still she could not see his face clearly but his build was slight, no bigger than Gavin and his legs—confounding her belief that he must be a city fella—were bowed in that country way, shaped from years astride a saddle or cattle bike. It was a knife he carried, polished and lethal. He stopped for a moment, indulging her futile efforts to evade him, then, invisible as a striking snake, he grabbed the child by his Peter Rabbit jumpsuit and plucked him from Cath's arms.

Cath looked down to where her arms still cradled the empty space. Below, her naked legs shimmered ghostlike and unfamiliar and from between them swung a thick, mucoid cord. Blue and twisted like a telephone cord. Cath traced its length to where Hughie lay gurgling in the man's arms, to where it disappeared between the poppers of his jumpsuit. She felt a slight tugging inside her womb as the cord tautened when the man, raising his knife, pulled Hughie further from her. Cath opened her mouth to scream but the cord was severed before she had time to fill her lungs. For a moment both ends fell slack. Then, like garden hoses animated by the full force of water, they each assumed a life of their own, flailing and whipping the air as a stream of blood spewed forth. Cath felt nothing, no pain and neither, she noticed, did Hughie who, still kicking enthusiastically, was now sucking on a bottle and gazing into the man's face. A face, now exposed to the light, she recognised. Gavin's face. He was rocking and cooing to his son, as if coaxing him back to sleep. As if they were quite alone in the room. Hughie reached up and pulled his father's nose in a way that had been exclusively hers. Then his arm fell limp and his legs gradually relaxed until there was no movement bar the odd twitch of his toes. The flow of blood from the cord slowed to a trickle, and finally Hughie closed his eyes.

Cath watched Hughie go without a flutter of alarm. She had more blood to spill but knew she was only seconds from following him. Seconds from being reunited. But how quickly Hughie seemed to have left the room. Gavin, still foolishly rocking away, seemed to hold nothing more than a stiff porcelain doll in a Peter Rabbit jumpsuit. Hughie was gone, probably somewhere over the cattle yards by now. For a moment Cath worried that, now he was free, he might not wait for her, might not need her anymore and she pushed down on her pelvic muscles to

force the blood through faster. He'd probably be over
Lotus Creek by now. That's where he'd wait for her.
Surely. That's where they always went together. To see
the butterflies. He loved to see the butterflies, thousands
of them rising, parting and beckoning like yellow clouds
as you passed by. But there were crocodiles too. They
could hide and ambush you if you didn't know where to
look, if you couldn't recognise a fresh spoor or if you got
between their nests and the water. Quick now, she must
hurry, he would need her to show him the way through.
She must hurry before the butterflies beguiled him, showed
him how to spread his wings and fly away. But the blood
kept coming and coming. Her thighs were wet and stained
red but death seemed no closer. Frantic, Cath ran to the
open door and filling her lungs with air screamed into
the empty sky.

'Wait, wait, I'm coming, I'm coming!' Cath cried, throwing
herself forward in the bed. It wasn't dark at all. The light
from a large fairytale moon was lying like a fresh carpet
of snow over every surface in the room. Behind the bars
of his cot Cath could see that Hughie was sucking
peacefully at the teat of his new bottle. Cath held her
head. The butterflies were still there, only their wings
were made of steel and they were bashing against the
inside of her skull. She wanted to smash her head against
the wall until it split like a coconut, and set them free.
Maybe if she lay back on the pillow and kept still they

would settle, rest their beating wings. Gavin, woken by her cry, her little moans and whimpers, turned towards her and sliding his hand up over her breasts whispered through a sleepy smile, 'Ummm ... have a nice dream did you?' Cath flung his arm away and leaped to the far side of the bed as if a death adder had slithered up over her. Her breasts were full, infected, throbbing with poison. Gavin raised his head off the pillow and looked at her. 'What the hell did I do?'

Tears of milk slid from Cath's nipples and dropped onto the sheet.

SARA DOWSE
Connections around Childbirth

8 pm, 23 December 1958. Two stainless steel doors of the sort that memory provides, accurately or inaccurately, for every hospital I've been to before or since, open and close as my husband and I say goodbye. We are agonisingly slow at it. The elevator (which I have only recently come to know as a 'lift') has gone up and then down and then up again in the time it has taken us to effect our parting, charged as it is with a host of unspoken fears. At last, he hands me the small suitcase he's been carrying, we kiss, and I step inside. I watch him, trying to save that last glimpse of him, as the doors with the hospital-buffed surfaces close over him. For all I know it could be the last time we meet.

War? A re-run of *Casablanca* at the very least? No, nothing quite so portentous or dramatic. It was, on the contrary, all too commonplace.

The lift took me up to the second floor where I was to spend the rest of the evening watching the lights from my window and listening to the hum of traffic down on Oxford Street. There were tramlines on the road then but only the tram to Bondi was still running. The hot night air was still and damp, but the smell of carbolic acid and methylated spirits cut through it. I crawled onto the hospital bed and kept cool by resting as much of myself as I could on its iron bars, difficult for someone so pregnant. Too pregnant. The baby kicking merrily inside me (but protesting mightily, I guess, against the pressure of the iron bars) had waited long enough, and in the morning was getting an obstetrical shove.

The last weeks, the last one in particular, had been hideously uncomfortable, and I would have been glad they were coming to an end if it weren't for the fact that the prospect of delivery terrified me. Women died in childbirth—only too frequently in the books I read and in the movies to which I was addicted. There comes a time in every full-term pregnancy when you realise there is only one way out. Experience counts for little here, in fact may make it worse. But the kind of ignorance that was mine in 1958 doesn't help much either. I spent those last swollen weeks sailing, if it could be called that, on a ship from California, then in my in-laws' pub on Blues Point Road, and finally in a one-room flat in North Sydney. My mother-in-law put a layette together but the only information I had about childbirth came from the barmaid, Lil. She frightened the daylights out of me with stories about her birthing stool, a short-legged device with a hole in the middle which got her through two labours. Although it makes sense today when all of us know that it's better for a woman to squat than to lie flat on her back with her legs in a pair of stirrups, then it seemed a terrible contraption, quite medieval. Sweating on my bed in the labour ward I felt sure that this was the sort of thing that lay in store for me. I was in a strange country, where virtually anything could happen, and did. I'd already been confronted with inscrutable customs, such as the six o'clock swill and Saturday morning shopping.

This was Australia in the 1950s. My in-laws' pub was one of those old-fashioned red-brick and cream-tiled affairs that closed from six to seven o'clock in the evening so that the serious drinkers could at least take time off to eat. Their womenfolk would be waiting outside on the steps for them, shelling peas into saucepans balanced on their knees. Early the next morning the bar would be hosed down, and a new day's drinking would begin. There was no such thing as a pizza or sour cream or a supermarket; soon after my arrival I was handed a wicker shopping basket to make the daily trip for provisions around the shops in North Sydney. At noon on Saturdays everything except the pubs and the races shut down.

All this was a revelation to me, but my ignorance concerning sex and parturition is harder to understand

and all the more unbelievable given that I came from Hollywood, where childhood even then was lost to training bras and pre-pubescent dates. But on reflection this makes sense. The facts of life did not flow uncensored from the fantasy mill, and the emphasis was on sex, not parturition. Childbirth was either the death of the mother or a piece of cake. It took Australia to put me straight. I came here thinking I was sophisticated. Everything seemed slow and unnecessarily complicated to me then, including my baby. I was impatient for life, but Hollywood prepares you for little other than a replication of itself. Smouldering heroines, gun-toting outlaws—there was even a place for high-jinks romance, those slanging-match comedies where women hurled insults at men and men hurled them back, in an elaborate disguise of their passion. Through this indoctrination I came to believe that slanging-off *was* passion, a view which needless to say landed me in a whole heap of trouble.

But when I say I was impatient for life I see now that I was impatient for passion. Or perhaps what I wanted was intensity of feeling. First-hand, unmediated feeling. Eros is what I would call this now, a specific orientation, charged with sex, which sometimes but not always is expressed in a sexual fashion. It certainly is not tied to procreation—any priest, any madam, any novelist under thirty could tell you that. But just as the current emphasis on the body in cultural debate might be seen as a reaction to the dominance of theory, I suspect that my embrace of this young pregnancy, when everything about my life before it seemed to be pointing in a different direction, represents a similar tribute to Eros. For someone so informed and influenced by fantasy, pregnancy, and all the bodily changes associated with it—the swollen breasts, the darkened nipples, the retching, the stretchmarks—was *real*. It seems the more our lives are directed by the intellect and technology, and the more we experience life vicariously, the greater is our need for asserting our own quite humble but wondrous corporeality.

Not long after I took to that iron hospital bed, waiting for birth to be induced the following morning, my labour began spontaneously. When the pain started getting strong I rang the bell for the nurse and asked for an aspirin, thinking I was having those false contractions that come late in pregnancy, and which matched in intensity the pain I had had each time I got my period. But the nurse felt around and said, 'No, you're in labour, silly', and led me off to the delivery room, where I was immediately strapped onto a table and dressed in starched green cotton.

The labour lasted over twenty-four hours. It hurt but I don't remember much more about it except how wonderful the nurses were, though they were perfect strangers and were only performing, after all, what was their professional duty. Yet in the dim light of the delivery room they held my hand, joked with me, gave me nitrous oxide when it looked like I needed it. Then the doctor came, my local GP, who nonetheless had delivered many babies. I can't remember what he said but I do remember his voice and a bright lamp shining into my eyes and down on the shaved pudenda between my outstretched legs and another mask being put to my face, only this time the gas was ether. I woke up the next morning puzzled by my flat stomach and asked whether I had had a baby. The doctor, who was either still there or had come back, said that yes, I'd had a baby boy.

A couple of years ago I was privileged to be witness to the birth of my first grandson. Times have changed enormously since my husband and I parted so awkwardly at the lift. My daughter had chosen the birthing centre at the very same hospital; it was a tiny cottage separated from the main building by a catwalk and several thousand light years in outlook. Not only was her partner there to help her but I was as well; the entire population of Sydney could have been present had she wanted. Deep in labour, she was free to move about the centre, from the bath to the mock-up bedroom. Instead of the green starched top and leggings I had been encased in, my daughter was stark naked. Instead of the sweet-smiling stoicism required of me, she had been exhorted by everyone from Sheila Kitzinger down to holler her head off if she needed to. Indeed, the first sound I heard when I rushed into the centre was that of my daughter screaming. Because for all this progress my daughter was in a good deal of pain.

I would not wish to arrogate that pain to myself, or

suggest that throughout those anguished hours I would have for a moment changed places with her. Yet I have to say that the experience was harrowing for me. To feel helpless in the face of someone else's pain is harrowing, especially if it is someone you love. At one stage it got so bad that I had to leave the room, and in the corridor I approached the midwife and muttered something traitorous like 'Who would be a woman?' It was quite the wrong thing to say. The birth centre was a recent victory, the outcome of a feminist campaign to wrest back control over childbirth, and so much as an intimation that women might still be victims in all this was tantamount to heresy. Meanwhile my daughter was suffering, all the more as the night wore on, but she refused the pethidine. No drugs! Again, I risked opprobrium by asking if she would use the gas, and to this she agreed. The midwife wheeled in the cylinder of nitrous oxide and put me in charge of administering it. Down on my hands and knees, bending over my daughter who was now on the floor on a mat, I showed her how to place the mask over her mouth and inhale over the contractions, which were coming thick and fast. It was the first time that night I felt even slightly useful, although I knew that the gas works as a distraction and hardly ever reduces the pain.

All through her thirty-six hour labour my daughter changed position. She squatted, grasping the maple foot of the double bed. She lay on her side on the mat. She stood upright, majestically spreading her arms and legs.

She swore, she quipped, she howled. Yet even as all this was happening I was struck by how beautiful she looked, with her dark skin, her blooming cheeks, her shining black hair and eyes. It didn't seem right. All this suffering—and beauty?

The baby, a boy like my first, was born at eight o'clock in the morning. His head had crowned two hours earlier, and the suspense of those two hours was like nothing I have experienced. Never in my most extreme imaginings, tense with fear on that iron bed thirty-four years before, did I dream that one day I'd be down on the floor only a few metres away, peering at my own daughter's vagina, and praying for her baby to come out.

Why do we do it? Surely this is the time to consider that we are driven by larger powers. Why else subject ourselves to so much trauma? Yes, I know, there are those of us for whom birth is nothing: a couple of hours, some discomfort, and that's that. There are those for whom it's quite the largest orgasm they've had. But for most of us, it's difficult; a compulsion perhaps to begin with, that conception so many months before, but nine months later even more so. Delivering a child from out of one's own body, at one and the same time the most personal, yet most social and universal of processes, we are swept up in forces larger than ourselves. Learning this can be a brutal discovery. My daughter's beauty was a paradox, but Eros is a complex god.

A woman has to deliver and a baby struggles to get

born. While everything is designed to effect this first, archetypal passage—the softening and parting of the mother's pelvic bones, the elasticity of the birth canal and its forceful, rhythmic contractions—it is a bumpy ride, beset with perils. This largely somnolent sybarite, if at times impatient or playful, is suddenly thrust with little preparation into the most serious business of its life. Until then it's been spinning cartwheels in a private pool, warmed to a glowing heat, as if anticipating the sun. When the time comes, determined by who knows what clock, this self-indulgent voluptuary mustn't get it wrong. If it manages to position itself properly, its head the advance party, instead of finding itself being dragged down by its feet, and if it manages to escape the tangle of the cord and prevent it becoming a tourniquet round its neck, it might succeed. One false move, though, and it's done for. What siren songs lure the child on, out of its sweet, contemplative womb-life to the struggle for existence beyond? This may be the central accomplishment of life, besides which all our puny strivings pale. And yet it goes largely unchronicled.

In Patricia Grimshaw, Marilyn Lake, Ann McGrath and Marian Quartly's stunning history, *Creating a Nation*, the opening event is just such an act. 'We do not know the date on the Christian calendar, but some time after the beginning of 1791', the authors write, 'Warreweer, a woman of the Wangal clan and Eora people, went into labour at the township of Sydney Cove.' She was attended

117

by two female kin, one of whom would pour cold water on her abdomen to 'soothe and comfort her'. The other eased the pain by transference, tying 'a small line' around Warreweer's neck and rubbing her own lips on the end of it till they bled.

The women sang birthing songs to embolden her. Her husband was not with her, but from a distance she could hear him singing. Warreweer's attendants did not intervene in the actual birth, would not 'touch her genitals or the baby's head'. Her position was upright, probably squatting, and when the baby pushed through, it dropped on the hollowed earth 'prepared with a soft bed of bark and leaves'.

Some British women who were present cut the umbilical cord, which seemed to the Aboriginal women an abrupt, even cruel thing to do. To them the cord had special powers and cutting it too short risked the infant's life. A smaller hole awaited the placenta: 'its burial . . . linked mother, child and land.' Then the British women washed the baby, where the Aboriginal women would have rubbed it with sand. Warreweer herself was 'smoked' with herbs to help stop her bleeding and to encourage her milk.

How wonderful to begin a history with an account of something as humble as this birth. That it serves a symbolic function, foreshadowing many of the problems which were to plague the nation in its adulthood, cannot obscure the profound shift in approach. No planting of ensigns on foreign shores, no cannon's boom, no signing of documents, no con. Just a birth. But once it occurred nothing was ever the same. For Warreweer and her people, for the land they were part of, everything, ineluctably, would change.

Looking again at the vastly different births experienced by the babies born to Warreweer, my daughter and to me, I see that life is a constant, and yet is constantly changing. This land was witness to all three, and the land has altered, down to the minutest particulars. The cove as it was in Warreweer's time is gone; in its place are container ships and an Opera House and other tall buildings of glass and steel and concrete. A short distance away is the hospital where my son was born, and the birth centre, scene of my daughter's labour. The baby born to Warreweer entered a bark cocoon after its exertions, only to be shocked by the swift, unanaesthetised severing of its cord. As the chroniclers of its birth record, the impact of change was already making itself felt on this tiny person; the British women present seem like some auguring chorus, uninvited but prophetic, like the witches in *Macbeth*. My first son was pulled by steel forceps out of a body rendered unconscious by the desperate application of ether after a labour of more than twenty-four hours. Whoever it was who first held him was a stranger, not only to him but to me. His feeding, fixed to a four-hourly schedule, began at three in the morning when he was wheeled in from the nursery. It was Christmas, half the nurses were on leave, and mothers and babies were

119

continuously awakened or interrupted so the straitened rump could get through their chores. The bonding of mothers and infants was subordinated to an efficient if inflexible hospital bureaucracy. The woman I shared a room with, a doctor herself, finally pulled rank and went home, leaving her infant so she could get a few days' rest. I saw my baby too seldom to establish good nursing, but my ever-ballooning breasts were expected to respond to a diabolic electric sucking machine. My grandson, on the other hand, was never separated from his mother and was encouraged to suckle when he pleased.

What sort of civilisations imprinted themselves on these infants? What civilisations will they in turn create? When I was younger I imagined that childbirth was incidental, almost irrelevant to achievements of the intellect, to industry, commerce, or politics. But this response itself was only indicative of a culture which either ignored or devalued both women and bodies. Even today there is a danger that as we give voice to our experiences as living, physical, female beings, however important or powerful these experiences may be, they will continue to be locked out of history, and only those which mirror the activities of men will be admitted. Now that I am a grandmother I have come to see childbirth as a central, revelatory event. It takes a new imagination to see this, the knitting together of body and mind, severed long ago with a thrust every bit as cruel and insensitive as the cutting of Warreweer's baby's cord. In a very real sense we human beings are connected to each other, and to the lands that sustain us; are connected through time, by these cords, and we would do well to respect them. Starting with a fumbling in the dark, the drive to orgasm of Shakespeare's beast with two backs, human life is born and, as a result, the world as we know it, is too.

Reference:

Patricia Grimshaw, Marilyn Lake, Ann McGrath and Marian Quartly, *Creating a Nation: 1788–1900*, Ringwood, McPhee Gribble, 1994.

ANNA BOOTH
Balancing Act

As I drive away from home on a Monday morning to catch the familiar Qantas 7.35 am flight to Melbourne, I experience the same feelings: a preoccupation with timetable and tasks to be completed, overwhelmed by a muddle of loss and anxiety at leaving my 'babies'. Blokes have been kissing their families goodbye for centuries and heading off to work and war, yet I never have the kind of conversations with them that I frequently have with mothers about leaving their children. Maternal instincts do exist!

I remember very clearly the precise moment when my decision to have a child was crystallised; but I have no recollection of the passage of that decision, or of when I began to contemplate motherhood, weighing the pros and cons, or imagining the consequences for my life and my relationship with my husband. I just recall a revelation one winter evening—I wanted to have a baby. My husband must have seen it coming because his response was unfussed and laid back, rather like my husband is in most circumstances.

'Well,' he said, as I snuggled up to him in front of the fire with a glass of champagne in my hand, 'if you want a belly full of arms and legs, I suppose we'd better arrange it.' I promise you, his exact words. I cried, poured another glass of champagne, and went into the bathroom and threw my contraceptive pills into the bin.

I gave up alcohol the next day and expected to be pregnant the next week. It was such a momentous decision for me. I felt like telling everyone as one would when actually pregnant. But I had never seen myself as a parent. I was thoroughly immersed in my job as a trade union official. I had always responded to questions about the biological clock with disdain. Once it was suggested that I shouldn't be a candidate for the most senior position in my union because I might 'get pregnant' (as it was put). My response was a flippant one. 'If I get pregnant, I'll have an abortion.' These words, which I regret saying with such carelessness, haunted me as the months turned into years before I fell pregnant. I convinced myself I had so abused my body that I was infertile. When I visited the gynaecologist for tests, time and denial had overtaken my initial zeal and no one was more shocked than I to discover I was, at last, pregnant.

Five years on I am the mother of two great kids and have decided to leave the job that really, at one time, consumed my life. Not that I want to withdraw from the workforce altogether, I don't. But I do want a job that allows more give and take, a better fit between my working life and my family life.

I just delight in the role of 'mother'. I like the word, I relish the stereotype. I enjoy the 'chat' about parenting with others, particularly mothers. I find common ground with women I would have once regarded as 'the enemy'. The pregnant human resource manager of a company I'm in an industrial dispute with becomes a 'chum'; the mother who is a National Party member of parliament, my 'soul mate'! It's so challenging, it's a totally new side of me I never knew could exist.

I've rediscovered extremes of emotion I remember from puberty and I thought were behind me. I'd thought I'd matured, thought, 'I'm tolerant, a measured rational life is fine.' All this is now forgotten! The love—I have never felt such deep love or such fear, especially the fear of rejection. I am flabbergasted that I agonise over whether my children really love me; and the fear of harm coming to them, the prospect of danger befalling them, sends me into a blind panic.

And gender, I've discovered gender and nature. My politically correct behaviourist-oriented views are over-taken by what I see before my very eyes—boys and girls are different (inside as well as outside) and I love the way my son and daughter interact differently with me and my husband.

I see the tremendous importance of the bond between us all as social glue as much as the personal reward that it constitutes. We have a special, extra dimension to this as one set of our children's grandparents lives with us.

And I have changed in many ways too. I feel that I now understand in a way that I never did before I had children, how critical self-esteem is. Even at the earliest age, how fundamental to good character and happiness is a sense of belonging, or origin, of place in the world. I hear my four-year-old son Angus constantly referring to our 'family' and in that he includes not just everyone in our household but my husband's sister and her family who live far away in Perth. We only see them once in a blue moon. But he knows they exist and he understands their relationship to us and where he fits into that jigsaw. It is of great importance to him that the jigsaw exists, and that he is part of it.

I believe it is necessary to put a great deal of effort into establishing these relationships and maintaining them. It is not simply that he is a part of the family, but that this is reinforced on a daily basis by the presence of the people who matter to him and are involved in both trivial and important parts of his day. I'm convinced that active parenting by both mother and father is of great significance to the development of a child. Perhaps ironically, I think my working full-time actually enhances the relationship that both my husband and I have with our children. I have become involved in Angus's kindergarten parents' committee, and through that I have seen a number of different approaches to parenting. I see parents where the male spouse works full-time and the female spouse works part-time or does not work at all, and where the husband is an absentee parent working long hours during the week and removing himself from the family for a good part of the weekend for sporting commitments.

I have recently faced the choice myself of opting out of full-time work to pursue part-time work and spend more time with the children. I've chosen to remain in a full-time job, not one that will be as demanding as my occupation as a trade union official, but nevertheless a serious executive role in a public company. I'm not completely sure it's the right choice. I know there will be times when I kick myself but I just love to work—love getting my hands dirty, being part of a team, getting the job done. I think I'm a better mother, wife, friend and daughter when I am a full-time worker, so I'm destined to continue this balancing act and deal with the paradox of feelings and frustrations—the joy that is the juggle between work and family.

It is important, I think, to be demanding about the accommodations that others must make to permit this balancing act to work. I think it's the single biggest feminist issue and the major reason for the existence of the glass ceiling or, as Anne Keating, general manager of an airline company puts it, the 'sticky floor'. It is when women assume full responsibility for the maintenance of the family, and then attempt to play by the corporate rules set by male executives *for* male executives, that they come unstuck and opt out for a quieter life.

Men and women who want a saner relationship between their commitments to family and work must bring their needs to others' attention. Often I think they will find that changes can be made to things like meeting times, conference venues and travel requirements, which others, without the demand of a family, have simply not thought to address.

The glass ceiling exists, make no mistake about it. It is not a figment of feminist imagination. Only a handful of senior executives are women with fewer still making it to the ranks of chief executive officer. That is not so imponderable, really. In other millenia, biology and the harsh environment meant women bore, nurtured and raised children while men hunted and defended. Both roles were all-consuming with no time available to mix them. As the centuries changed the mode of fulfilling these roles changed and men occupied positions of power and status in the church, the military, politics and business. They understood each other. Even your enemy was able to second-guess you because he was your gender. There is little wonder that having occupied these positions there is a certain lack of enthusiasm about allowing women in. It creates discomfort, introduces unpredictability and yes, even the distraction of sexual attraction.

Most of my experience, whether in the trade union movement or in business, is of men who are married to women who are not in the paid workforce and who have borne and nurtured their two-point-something children. On the whole these men have been caring fathers but have not by any stretch of the imagination shared parenting. They have worked long hours, travelled frequently and taken enormously difficult decisions with the support—practical and emotional—of women who have cooked, cleaned and arranged their domestic lives for them.

The first wave of female executives were, by and large, unmarried or married and childless, and they accepted these rules. They had to survive. They worked long hours, travelled frequently and made enormously difficult decisions with the support of paid services to cook, clean and arrange *their* domestic lives. For many of these women their close relationships were with other women. At work they didn't challenge the paradigm that they became 'one of the boys'. The second wave of women who want to get to the top face a different challenge. They are married with children and the rules don't suit them at all. Neither do the rules suit the men they are married to.

I think there is a revolution occurring in corporate Australia and it's driven by men and women who want to spend time with their families. They are prepared to work hard and achieve, but they want understanding. They want room for the unexpected to occur without

129

judgement. And they want to forget things like team-building breakfasts.

One of the most difficult things I find about being a parent, particularly a working parent, is finding time for myself and for my husband and I to be together. Children don't know when to stop, so we have to tell them; but when time is limited that becomes a guilt trip. I've seen what I think are mistakes made by other working parents who let their children stay up late at night because it is the only time during the working week that they get to see them. But the legacy is one of undisciplined kids who don't have a sense of boundaries. I seek refuge from the questions and the demands and the desires of my children at five in the morning in the shower, blow-drying my hair, in the car on the way to work, at the airport lounge and occasionally in the gym.

This is the other side of the work and family thing. I find work a refuge, not just an occupation for earning income, but a place where I can relax and regain some control. I like the structure that it gives my life. I often hear women, particularly, say, 'Oh you must be so organised to have a family and go to work. I find that I start the day with lots of jobs and only get a few of them done.' I can understand that. When I was on maternity leave after the birth of my daughter Clare, I found the day just slipped past. I hadn't achieved a great deal and I found it frustrating. Now that I am back in full-time work I still do the basic chores but I can also do eight or nine hours in the office and find that tremendously satisfying.

I guess the most important thing of all is to enjoy the time with my children and my time at work—not to be thinking about one whilst doing the other. I'm constantly amazed at the richness of life. Sitting in the park watching my children playing in the sandpit, I feel like the luckiest person alive. Of course they grow up, and I want to have strong memories of their childhood so I work at saving time for being with them. Saying no has become an art-form. Are there are downsides to this balancing act? Yes, not enough sleep. By my reckoning I should catch up on that in about 2003.

SUE WOOLFE

Ghosts

G*randma's house*
Tuesday maybe

Dear mum,

Yesterday there was a knock on the door. You'll remember how exciting a doorknock is here. I was dreading Ernie. I sort of tidied up on the way to the door to show I'm coping. I'm glad I did. It was Steve from the next gully. We'd met in the supermarket. I'd been rushing my trolley around a corner because the baby was yelling. He'd offered to hold the baby at the checkout while I fished for my purse down the bottom of the bag under three nappies, not folded, all tangled. Then the purse zipper caught in a thread and wouldn't break free.

Are you managing? he'd asked. I was trying to unpick the zipper. The shop assistant was sighing with the customers behind me and making a din on the counter drumming her fingernails.

But my eyes negotiated his, their exact and trembling circumferences. Neither of us breathed for a moment, that moment when men and women work out what to do with each other next.

I can imagine how your lips would tighten if you read this. She's not only picking up men in the supermarket, she's being disorganised in front of them as well, you'd think.

I got the zipper undone.

Yes, I'm managing, I said.

He'd driven me home all the same, peering out his mist-spotted windscreen at grandma's house.

Didn't some weird people live here? he'd asked.

Yes, they did. My grandmother.

I shouted over my shoulder, running up the drive with my bundled baby and my shopping, and trying to wave. He didn't start his car till I'd put on the lights.

Today he brought around a bunch of egg and bacon flowers.

How lovely, I said, although grandma's garden is so overgrown with egg and bacon flowers, I've been hacking them to oblivion.

Can I come in? he asked.

He was gazing around at the walls and ceiling.

My mother is sure this house has ghosts, he said.

I hoped he wasn't going to talk about his mother much. He's got that shiny, scrubbed look of a man who talks about his mother.

His eyes were on me, fingering me like another question.

My grandmother died here, I offered.

I kept laughing in his company, as if at any moment there'd be a party.

Then the baby murmured, distracting us both.

Look, I said. She's discovered her mouth.

Her mouth is a triangle with a little indentation on the base. You haven't seen it yet of course. She moved it to one side.

She looks like a cowboy villain talking out of the corner of his lips, Steve said.

Back to the middle, to rest. Then to the other side. Back again. A pause. Then the upper lip curled. In contempt for me? I wondered and my heart pounded. But the mouth came back to rest. Then she smiled.

She only smiled by chance, I told Steve, but I was hoping.

Have you always wanted a baby? asked Steve.

He's going to ask many questions.

He told me he grew up in an extended family. They took it in turns for years to hold his fretting younger brother.

No, I said.

Even my teeth sounded savage as I answered. All the time I was growing up, I swore I was finished with families.

I'm wasting so much time, I can't leave her cradle. Five metres away, and she's asleep and my manuscript is on my lap. I stare out the huge windows at the misty bush that's all around us. I blink at it without wonder, like a goldfish. All I want is to be immersed in her.

I had to hint to Steve to go home, otherwise he might've lounged by the fire all afternoon, the firelight dancing over his jumper. I didn't want to breastfeed in front of him. He would deliberately not watch. Then ask to stay the night.

Several times he turned to see if I was waving to him. Each time we waved. Around him, snow was falling more urgently than whispers.

Of course I can't ever send you this. There are many things we've never said to each other. Between a mother and daughter, birth is an immaculate conception. But it helps me to think about you, writing like this. You were always so distant in my childhood. You weren't distant with grandma. Remember when grandma told you I wasn't to sleep in your bed? That was the end of our warm toasty nights. Remember when she said that I was to stop learning the piano because I was taking it too seriously? That I wasn't to have a dog?

Yes mum, you'd say to her, and obey, whatever my feelings. Were you apologising to her for her life, as if it was your fault?

Was it your fault?

It's as if in these letters I'm constructing you bit by bit, a jigsaw, and maybe the picture I'm constructing isn't you at all.

A couple of days later

I woke before her bird cries, to pat the sheets beside me. I'd been dreaming of Steve, dreaming he lay in my bed. My hand gathered their lonely folds. Stay and keep me warm, I think I'd say if my hand ever gets to cradle him. I'll swap sex for warm, toasty nights.

Then Zoe my bird sang out, and I didn't think again till now.

Maybe next day

A car in the drive. I've brought Steve here by wishing, my heart sang. I left Zoe on my bed and grabbed a dress from the wardrobe before he knocked. I hadn't got out of my nightie for days. Suddenly I remembered I hadn't washed or combed my hair. But he didn't knock, and I was stuck with my head through the neck of the dress when I heard breathing in the doorway. I yanked the dress on. Ernie was standing there.

Thought I'd see how you were going, he said.

You've never seen him, you don't know what he looks like. His hair stands up from his scalp, fading into blondness before it falls on his forehead. His freckles are paler in winter. He'd ironed his collar—I noticed that immediately, and that he'd ironed wrinkles into the points.

I thought I'd see how you both were getting on, he said into the silence of the bedroom.

It was the first time I'd seen him since the hospital. He came over and leaned to look at Zoe. She was big-eyed on my bed. He was smiling his easy smile. He was polite enough to edge his back to me so I could scramble into my dress properly.

Gee willikins, he said, gazing at her.

I'd forgotten he says gee willikins. It rocketed through me as it did when I first met him. My jaw clenched. My mind paled. How could I have gone to bed with someone who says gee willikins?

I picked up a clean nappy and moved so he had to stand aside. My fingers were long and dextrous on the nappy folding. I was showing off. But then the nappy pin jammed.

Allow me, he said.

I'm okay, I said. I jerked it out and rubbed it in my hair but it still jammed. I gave it such a fierce push it missed the nappy fold but pierced my thumb. I tucked the nappy end around her waist and held her tight so it wouldn't fall off. I hoped blood wasn't dripping. Then of course he wanted to hold her.

She has to go to sleep now, I said.

I took her out to her cot.

Can you make us a cup of tea? I asked, to get him out of the room so I could wrap up my finger.

I was rocking her despite her grizzles. Her eyelids closed, fluttered open. Too late I remembered I'd run out of tea. In the kitchen, I could hear water streaming into the sink over three days of my unwashed dishes.

He opened the door to whisper, Are you out of detergent?

What's wrong with soap? I whispered back.

He shut the door. Perhaps I drowsed then, but my hands have learned to rock her while I drowse. My anger returned in a clatter of dishes. I went out to the kitchen to tell him to be quiet. But the workbenches were gleaming as if the sun was out, the dishes were stacked as white and innocent as flowers, the floor was swept, the whole kitchen was smiling and he was pouring tea from grandma's old teapot. He'd brought an electric heater and turned it on.

In case you'd run out of firewood, he said.

So that's why the sun seemed to be shining.

I brought you some tea, a special blend, he said. And chocolate Tim Tams.

He'd started eating, he was already licking smears of chocolate from his fingers.

139

Chocolate's bad for breast milk, I said.

He kept the packet open, he kept eating them. I could just see the edge of a biscuit at the end of the rip. So I had no choice. I gobbled three biscuits without stopping, dropping chocolate crumbs on the tabletop that was gleaming as peacefully as a body of water between us.

I'll go up and buy another packet, he said as I finished the chocolate biscuits.

They're bad for breast milk, I said again, but he didn't seem to notice.

You could get biscuits without chocolate, I said.

But I like chocolate, he said.

There was a pause.

I'm glad you're doing fine, he said, smiling without irony. Perhaps there was a droop of sadness at the corner of his lips.

A second cup? he asked. I'll put the kettle on again. All that work has made me thirsty.

I walked out into the yard and noticed for the first time that it was littered with wood chips from my daily chopping for the fire. He followed me out.

Something's happened to the chopping block, he said. Gee willikins, it's split in two.

You wouldn't know, but when you've got a baby, you're always in a hurry, I said.

He went back for the kettle screeching on the stove, creeping the door shut behind him. He came back with our tea.

140

I panicked after she was born, he said, as if that was an explanation.

I wish I could've, I said.

I've been sleeping on people's sofas, he said. And wondering.

I threw my dregs into the bushes. He did the same. The drops arched and fell. For a moment, they mirrored the sullen sky.

He laughed suddenly. He always laughs like that, before he explains.

See this tip on my nose? The way it sticks out? Like a little roof? he said.

He angled his head to show me his profile against the trees. He's twenty-three, but it's still a little boy's profile with a freckled nose.

See? There?

I moved my feet on the cold earth. I'd forgotten to change out of my slippers.

Why are we talking about your nose? I asked.

His eyes surprised me, they were so glossy in that grey air. Suddenly they were overflowing and tears ran down his face.

Because she's got my nose, he said. My nose has been re-created in her.

He dug a crumpled handkerchief out of his pocket to wipe his face.

I'm going inside, I said. Don't follow me, it's over.

I was at the kitchen steps, I'd just reached the door

handle when he called, We could take turns with the baby.

My hand slid on the frozen door handle. It was too cold to hold onto.

You could get on with your writing, he added.

My breath tunnelled steam into the icy air.

You could be a writer as well as a mother, he said.

In the silence, a bird called.

Get lost, I said. I don't need anyone.

Love,
Sally

Grandma's house
Wednesday

Dear mum,

I'm sitting in grandma's sunny bush garden and the writing's coming easily as if someone smarter than me is inside my head. The nappies leap on the washing line strung between the gum trees and it's so quiet I can hear a bird's wing fluttering, the crackle of twigs as leaves drop. Even the washing basket near the open door looks like peace. I think about that other child inside me, my heroine. Maybe, maybe, it's possible to be both a mother and a writer.

Bits of a new character drift in. People talk to her and I write down what they say. I'm not sure where they're talking, so I manufacture bedrooms, bedsheets, tables, apple cores, lips, verandahs, candles, even people's feet, all in the most cavalier way. I go from elation to horror at the presumption of it, but I must write on. It's leading me. I follow. I'm trying to map this bewildering landscape inside my head. She's unwinding in me, my heroine. I love her. In the haze of my mind she twitches and glows.

There were moments when you'd shake yourself free, and remember that you were a mother as well as a daughter.

What shall we do today? you'd ask.

So the sun would pour golden liquid into the room and swirl while I stroked your hand and tried not to cling to it. If I clung softly, you mightn't retreat.

You always retreated.

Your mother was your first, your only love.

Another letter I won't send. But it's such a comfort.

Definitely Friday

She's got a rash, she's spewing her milk, she isn't hungry. I gave her another bottle of boiled water while we watched the evening come down over the bush. Her eyes closed over the sucking at last and I nodded a little with her. It isn't important to be a writer.

She cried in the night.

In the velvety silence of night, terror has a shape. It's your half-closed eyes one afternoon in the laundry at home. I was about ten years old, and it was one of those brown-hazed Sydney summers when everything sticks to the skin. I was looking through the crack in the laundry door. You didn't lift your eyes from the grey laundry floor where puddles of water slowly dried. Your half-closed eyes were like crescent moons in the middle of the brown day. You didn't care that it was Sunday, that we could run across the green park or catch a ferry and watch the waves scurrying like people head down in a subway. When I called you didn't hear me any more, you leaned against the washing machine all afternoon, watching puddles of grey water dry.

Did you learn that from grandma? And did grandma learn it from her mother? And her mother? Is this our dreadful inheritance, that the women of our family live as if we're stranded in the wrong life, dumped?

In the black night my fists are clenched so tight, the blood in them flows yellow hot, and I say what all daughters of sad mothers say: I will never, never be like her.

Did you say that?

It wasn't my fault you were so sad. Was it?

Love,
Sally

Grandma's house
Sunday

Dear mum,

Days are reckoned good or bad now by how long the baby sleeps. But who can I tell my secret thoughts to? Only you. I can't let you see who I am. She's waking up. She wakes with her bird cries at the merest whisper of my pencil. I'm raging but I must go to her.

Am I the only resentful mother in the . . .

Grandma's house
Monday 15

Dear mum,

Zoe slept. I sat near her cradle and rocked. With assiduous rocking, she slept till five in the afternoon. I'm up to page ninety of this draft and I'm pretty pleased with myself. The manuscript is at least filling with words.

If I hardly have to mother at all, I'm a happy mother.

Grandma's house
Thursday 18

Dear mum,

Steve visited again. He was being a family man, holding Zoe up the window to see the valleys, the gold sandstone of cliffs, the sun scudding across miles of bushland. He held her so easily and she nestled into his warmth. Ernie wouldn't have held her like that. Well, he hasn't had much practice. I was folding nappies still warm from the sun. (I have to wash nappies because the nappy wash delivery man only comes once a fortnight. He says I'm lucky he'll come at all, the road's so rough. I keep running out of their nappies and using mine and I get muddled whose nappies are whose—I mean, one nappy looks very much like another, given a few stains—and then I end up washing the lot, theirs as well as mine!) I feel compelled to tell you the details as if I'm trying to convince you that I'm a good girl, in spite of Ernie and a baby. I felt good at the time, the soap-smelling nappies and my chilly hands flaring with sudden warmth.

Babies make a place feel like a home, said Steve.

I busied myself neatening the nappy stack.

There's something in her eye, said Steve.

I was fingering the nappies, thinking about the way the denim jeans curved into his bottom.

Look, said Steve. Quick. There really is something in her eye.

Suddenly I was at the window with him, grabbing her. She was looking at me, her blue eyes, the blue of the shadows in the mountains out the window. She was squinting.

There is.

It might be scratching her eyeball, he said. Let's ring my mother. She'd know what to do, he said.

His eyes stretched out to mine like arms.

If we don't get help, he said, the scratches might be permanent.

I ran across the room for the baby manual you sent when you heard I was pregnant. I knew even then that was the closest you'd come. My hands were clumsy with your pages. I was looking up Eyes. For once I was fast at the alphabet.

Lick it out, the manual said.

I raced to the end of your page.

... or call a doctor.

You could never bear to get things out of my eyes. Keep crying, the tears will wash it out, you'd say.

Her blue eyes were waiting for me, squinting, waiting.

I can't call a doctor or an ambulance, I said to her, to Steve, to myself. We're out in the bush, they won't come all the way out here for cotton wool in a baby's eye.

The muscles moved in Steve's shiny face. I thought: He's going to insist on his mother. I thought: Because I have a baby, he thinks I want a mothering life.

Fury made me remember: Zoe came out of me, there might be something about my saliva, it might be like hers, might be like the fluid in her eye; it might be what she needs.

And I'm a mother now, hers, her mother.

She might remember this moment all her life. The huge red absurd mouth descending. The slow semicircle as my face moved towards hers. At some point on that semicircle, her face blurred and disappeared. When I put out my tongue, it was calculation or instinct, I don't know how to tell.

My tongue, her eye. Wet curve on wet curve.

On the third lick, it came out, a long thread of cotton wool. I handed her back silently to Steve, went into the kitchen, shut the door, put on the kettle for a cup of tea, leaned on the stove and stared out the window at the sunlit bush.

After a while Steve knocked on the door. Zoe sat on his arm as pert as a parrot on a branch.

What's wrong? he asked.

I started moving again, rinsing out the teapot and getting down the tea. I poured the boiling water into the pot. The steam rose into my face and then my face was cold.

I've just figured something out, I said.

Steve waited, and then asked: What?

I'm a mother, I said.

We stared at each other.

It'll probably take a while, he said.

I was beginning to think he understood.

Love,

Grandma's house
Don't know the day

Dear mum,

You were probably a natural mother. Always in command, always sure, knowing, calm, unhappy. Unhappy. But that's because I disappointed you.

I'd disappoint you now even more. I'm struggling hourly.

It's there underneath everything, when I turn, when I open the door, when I clean my teeth, when I smile— there's a dull grey cramp.

I know what I'm doing for her will stay with her all her life. But I've got to get through the minutes. And minute to minute, it's unutterably trivial. Just a burp, a fart. Maybe she swallowed, might that be wind? Or just a gurgle? So how can anyone, anyone remember what's important when every minute is so trivial?

I carry Zoe through the morning, a morning as grey as me. When she laughs at me I can barely manage a smile. Only when she sleeps does something ease.

And then my novel comes streaming out in bright ribbons, and my heart leaps.

The next day

There must be someone else as desperate as me. Is everyone desperate but pretending? You weren't, of course. I should learn to knit, purl and plain, purl and plain, and not mind that my life has slowed to a twirl of wool.

This morning she laughed her toothless, open-mouthed laugh. Her meaningless laugh. It had the mockery of kookaburras.

Help me, I said to her.

I sat on the sofa, cradling her like a madonna would've. I know them so well, those old paintings. The madonna head slightly tipped to hear only the baby. The madonna eyes narrowed to see only the baby. Light shouts behind the madonna head, but she doesn't turn. Those madonnas are like ancestors you mock all your life till you're a mother. Then they feel like home.

I arranged my face in a madonna rapture. You would've done that naturally. Zoe sensed the gravity of the moment. She held my gaze.

With a bit of help from you, I'll become a proper mother, I said.

But my mind, that constant busybody, kept chattering. You need a new character in your story, it said.

You could have a look at the clock and see how many seconds have gone by, it said.

Zoe looked away. When she looked back, my rapturous madonna face was still there. She burst out crying.

I'll ring you tomorrow.

I must be so happy when I ring you that I almost don't need to ring you at all.

That's why I daren't ring, why I daren't post these letters. I need you so much.

This afternoon I learned to make a complete revolution of this house last four minutes, with stops at the goldfish, at the windows, at the clock, at the fire and at the oven to pretend there was something in it. I switched the oven light on and off, on and off. With seven revolutions of the house I can make thirty minutes pass.

You, who knew this house so well in your childhood, you must admit that was a kind of triumph.

Later

Last night a new character started speaking in my head as I pushed the stroller around the house. All day I'd been fighting with the dread. I turned the lights off and the room was striped in silver moonlight. Then in the quiet rhythm of the stroller wheels and the baby's head lolling heavy as a flower, the new character began to

151

speak. I had no feeling of effort, it was more a feeling of memory, of remembering. But I've never known anyone like this character. Her voice is gentle, wise, unscholarly and full of optimism. As I wheeled past the hallstand, I scribbled down what she was saying on a nappy wash receipt—there are always nappy wash receipts to write on in this house now, under milk bottles, in shopping bags, between the cushions on the sofa. But Zoe jolted awake and cried so I walked a few more rounds in grandma's silver house until she dropped back to sleep. Then the new character gave me the rest of the sentence. In her motherly way, she seemed prepared to wait.

This morning I read the words written last night in the moonlight and falling off the receipt and interrupting the computerised account number. She's put words to my feelings, words I couldn't find myself.

These days with a baby, I cry a lot. I stood on the lino floor in the kitchen with the nappy wash receipt in my hand and I was crying. Not for my baby, but for the character who understands me.

I wish she was you.

Love,
Sally

Grandma's house
Sunday

Dear mum,

Since you'll never read this, I can tell you about yesterday.

I'd taken Zoe out to the garden and we were watching leaves eddy and float. There were so many, they made a pattering on the ground. For a while I thought I'd come to a new peace, holding a baby to watch leaves. Before her, time fitted itself around my will. Now I must wait for the next leaf to fall.

And suddenly while I crunched leaves under my feet, Steve came swinging along the dusty road as easily as if I'd wished him there. In his arms he held a bunch of flowers again—potato creeper, another weed I've hacked out of grandma's garden. He's not good about flowers. But the sun was behind him and he was fringed with light.

I raced down the drive, Zoe chortling as I jolted.

You looked like an angel, I shouted before we stood smile to smile in the dusty road. Like the messenger angel who came to Mary. I've been wanting so much—

Hello, he said.

—to find out how you are, I've been wanting so much—words were blurting out of my mouth, I'm so unused to adult company these days—to talk. Have you come for a cup of tea? I asked.

Don't come near, he said. I've got a cough that won't go away, had it for weeks.

Nevertheless, he put his hands on my shoulders and breathed on Zoe and me.

So there he was in grandma's kitchen, his thin neck poking out of his sweatshirt. I could've reached out my fingers and caressed his skin's warmth, though I didn't, not yet. His eyelashes curl at the corners of his eyes, like the ones in make-up advertisements.

You've lost your tan, I said.

Winter, he said.

We both laughed, that it was winter, and that one day we might hold each other and our bodies would flare with warmth where they touch. It hung between us, this promise, like perfume. His neck muscles flexed handsomely as he put his flowers down on the sideboard.

Are they for me? I asked, surprised.

He picked them up and handed them to me, though I was holding Zoe.

I'll take her, he said. We laughed unnecessarily as we fumbled between the baby and the flowers.

She looks so comfortable with you, I said, though he was holding her the way she doesn't like, her legs astride his arm as if she was riding a horse. But it was true of the time he held her when he last visited. It wasn't really a lie.

Have the ghosts appeared in this house yet? he asked as the tap gushed water into the kettle.

No, I laughed.

I clanked cups, caught the kettle, measured tea leaves.

I remember how you have your tea, I said. I was so happy he was here, I could've almost chanted: milk with two sugars.

Cake! I shouted. I've just got a cake out of the oven!

For once I'd made a cake at the right time.

I must've known, he said, watching me.

I prised at it with a knife. It clung to the side of the tin.

Turn it upside down and bang, he said. That's what my mother does.

Your mother! I repeated, but I did what he said. The cake fell onto the plate, broken.

Doesn't matter, we'll pick at the crumbs, I said. This is going to be a real tea party.

I was pulling out drawers, finding grandma's tablecloth, her serviettes she never finished embroidering. I was shaking the mouldy years out of their creases.

He found a moth wing in one of the cups and showed Zoe how to blow it out. Then he held the other cup to her face and showed her how to blow into that one too.

Babies belong to all of us, he laughed. To the universe.

I loved him for that.

Sit down, sit down. I was waving him into a chair.

This is how my grandmother poured tea, I told him. She bossed us all into doing it like this.

I held the pot high and moved it down the stream of tea that winked amber in the light.

But I said, Her ghost is not going to get to me. She wound my mother around her finger, it used to make me mad. Because my grandmother was nothing, a nobody, she lived a life this size.

I showed the gap of a centimetre between my fingers before I passed him his cup.

I threw my arms out wide.

And I'm going to live a life this size.

Zoe flapped her arms in imitation like a flightless bird. But Steve was cutting the cake with serious jabs.

You've got a kid, he said.

As I write, I'm jabbing the paper with my pen—you can see the jabs. You were such a child with your mother, so ready to give her your life.

You called it love. That's why I wouldn't listen about your painting. Painting seemed only for the submissive. For the tiny.

Afterwards, while I was changing Zoe's nappy in the bedroom, Steve put his arms around my waist. His hand slipped so easily up to my breast, as if that's where it should've been.

Do you want me? he asked.

Desire stabbed me, there with my hands on the nappy table. I couldn't speak. I had to turn my back to him. It was hard to remember how to pin the nappy. I saw that Zoe's eyes were drowsed with milk, so I stumbled out of the room and put her back in her cot. When I came back, Steve was lying on the bed, on Ernie's side. I wasn't quite sure what to do. So I lay beside him. It seemed familyish.

Then Zoe began crying in her cot. I could hear it beyond his breath in my ear.

I won't take off my jumper, I said. As if that somehow made what I was doing less definite.

You're a prude, he said. I checked his face to see if he was joking, but I couldn't tell.

In case I have to run to her, I said.

She was really roaring now. But he'd unzipped his jeans. I didn't know him well enough to ask him to stop for a baby. I didn't like to ask him to touch me to excite me either. It would've taken up time and her screams were ripping the room. As it was, he came on my tummy, a puddle that was clammy so soon. He lay exhausted on top of me though he'd really done nothing. The room seemed full of his breath and her cries.

Then he mopped himself with the sheets and said: Aren't you worried about your baby crying? Don't you want to go and pick her up?

You say that now? I cried.

I threw him off and raced into her room. She was red and spongy, even her tiny scalp was crimson. When I picked her up, she screamed louder. It took twenty minutes to comfort her.

She might never forget that, he said. One day she might be on a psychoanalyst's couch saying, Once my mother let me cry while she fucked.

I was shaking with fury. I said, We both did it. Didn't you say babies belong to the universe?

He said, Ah! But you're her mother.

And of course he was right. It's as if I can't remember it. As if I can't remember who I am.

He was bent over, pulling jeans against the ripples of his stomach.

He said: You don't behave like a proper mother.

Who does? I sneered. Your mother?

We were shouting at each other, against Zoe's roars.

He struggled for the last word. He said, I don't understand how someone could treat her baby like that.

But I yelled at him as he got into his car:

Get lost.

I won't send you this.

Grandma's house
Sunday

Dear mum,

I've been trying to learn how to be a proper mum.

I opened the back door with Zoe strapped to me in her sling and the bush morning came in singing like a choir, the crickets and the currawongs and the whip birds and the wind from down the valleys. I trudged into it with the washing. I washed assiduously all morning, right down to the bottom of the laundry basket, to all the bits tumbling down there that get missed every wash, the old curtains and torn sheets and dusters and cloths to wipe things. When I pegged them to the dancing line with pegs they flapped wetly around Zoe and me.

Like a shroud, I told Zoe gloomily, though I'd never seen a shroud.

In the afternoon I sang to Zoe and told her stories. My voice went into her face and out the back of her head when she yawned. Together we watched the gum trees toss their heads wisely into the fading light. She slept and I dusted, I mopped, I swept. I brought the clothes in from the washing line. I took the iron out of the cupboard. A spider marched out of it defiantly. There were cobwebs between the handle and the temperature selector.

Next day

To be really consistent, I shouldn't keep writing to you. But it seems essential to tell you who I am, to find out who you are now I've got a daughter. So I will tell you that I fed the baby, I burped the baby, I put her to bed.

She was feverish. I didn't have a thermometer. All proper mothers have thermometers. In chemist shops, they don't buy lipsticks. They buy thermometers. It had never occurred to me to buy one. She snuffled in her sleep because of her cold. I cried as well. There didn't seem to be anything else to do. Just a long, slow forgetting. Her temperature dropped at dawn.

Sometime in the silent morning, I found Steve's phone number. I dialled the number. A woman answered. My heart paused, but no, her voice creaked with age.

Is Steve there? I asked.

No. Is that you, Karen? said the old woman's voice. He's been waiting in for days for you, and now he'll be sorry to miss you.

The wires clicked over my breathing.

No, it's not Karen, I said.

If you leave your name, I'll tell him you called, she said.

Tell him to keep his germs to himself, I said.

I hung up.

At night, after Zoe's last feed, I packed my manuscript into a big cardboard box. I stapled down the lid, and I put it away in the back of a cupboard.

Love,
Sally

Grandma's house
Tuesday

Dear mum,

All night she sneezed and coughed. Her skin was burning. I wondered how hot a little baby had to get before brain damage sets in. In the grey morning I rugged her up and rang for a taxi. I told him I needed a doctor.

I'll take you to the baby health clinic, the driver said.

I'd rather a doctor, I said.

I'd kept away from baby health clinics before. They're for women who can't cope.

My wife's on duty today, he said. We've brought up five of the little buggers.

I let him take me to the baby health clinic even though it wasn't open until nine. For a mother with a sick baby, nine o'clock is almost the end of the morning.

I was the first mother in line at the clinic, ahead of the women in silk blouses with babies in top-of-the-range Scandinavian strollers. For the first time, I noticed that Zoe's stroller was growing mould. Perhaps mould spores were getting into her lungs—maybe it wasn't Steve's germs after all. I remembered a tap in the garden near the clinic porch, and thought, perhaps I should go and wash the stroller right now under the tap, it might halt her deterioration. I was heading out the door to do this when

161

the sister called me in. I talked to her white hospital back as I followed her.

My baby's very sick.

Speaking about Zoe had become a feat of pitting my voice against the constriction of guilt in my throat.

Zoe fitted into the sister's big, comfortable arms.

What an absolutely perfect child, she said. To think we were once like this. Look at her, and what a picture of health.

She's getting worse and worse, I managed.

The sister looked up at me, startled.

What do you think is wrong? she asked.

My throat was a wall—words fell against it, then fell back. I looked around wildly. We were both standing up, she hadn't offered me a chair. I floundered around the room to find a chair. If I sat for a while, perhaps I could tell her how I've been betraying my baby not just with a man but with my writing.

She's got a cold, said the sister. You'd better get used to it. She'll have many in her life.

She handed Zoe back to me, went to a coffee machine, and brought back two polystyrene cups of coffee.

Sugar? she asked. Milk?

I nodded. Tears were running down my face; these days it seems normal to have a sheen of tears on my face. As she stirred my coffee, I noticed her arms were fat and fleshy, with a little point at the elbow. They were story-book arms that could be smeared with flour as they pulled a tray of hot sweet cakes from the oven for five children.

Sometimes, she said, the mums need a bit of mothering. My laugh was a wet snort in a tissue but she pretended not to notice. We drank our coffee in synchronous gulps. It was scorching our throats but I only had her reassuring presence for the length of time it took to drink a cup of coffee. Outside her door a dozen babies cried.

Is there anything you can do to mother yourself? she asked.

I've stopped doing it, I said.

Then start it again, she said. It'll give you strength. You mums need all the strength you can get, wherever you get it from.

She tossed her empty coffee cup across the room into her wastepaper bin with a practised hand, and stood up.

So the question blurted out of me.

How do I become a proper mother? I asked.

I've never met one, she laughed.

Her touch on my arm was as gentle as the movement of words in the mind, as gentle—how I remember with longing—as gentle as the nudge of Zoe when she was in the womb. As gentle as your cupping of my chin.

Everyone has to make it up as they go, she said.

All day I looked at people's faces in the street as I wheeled Zoe around the shops. I wanted to peer into their shopping bags, listen to their conversations, follow them home. I wanted to know how they made it up. Just before closing time I was considering carrots for dinner outside the green-grocer's. She had arranged fruit and vegetables in sunbursts against the glass window of the shop; yellow grapefruit for the sun and sticks of celery for the sun's rays.

You like? she asked me. She was smiling out of a brown felt face.

She laughed, and showed me the little wires she used to prop the sunbursts up.

Easy to do, she laughed. She patted my face.

Easy to be happy. Easy both to be happy. I show you. She plucked Zoe out of the stroller, held her high and said into her gummy smile:

I love you.

She put Zoe back in her stroller.

See? I made the words go right inside her.

As I walked away, there was a bleached white crescent moon in the sky, the shape of your sad eye. I put my basket down on the footpath and kneeled to show it to Zoe.

And then it came to me, as the grit of the footpath crunched under my shoes: Zoe, watching my face, is learning what I learned, your sad eyes, my mother whose life was as bleached as a moon in a sunny sky brilliant with promise.

Next day

Zoe woke and I fed her, but she drowsed on the breast, and all any mother can do is put a sleeping baby back in

164

her cot. The house waited in silence. The roof shifted in the afternoon sun. The silence waited for me. I took out a clean sheet of paper and typed a few words, my fingers stumbling on the unfamiliar keyboard. But there wasn't any more noise, not for a long, long time.

Next day

Today it allowed me back inside its cushioned softness, my story. I'm inside it and it's inside me. I've re-written the ending, astonishingly fast after months of anguish. Now I'm re-writing and suddenly it's easy. I float above the typewritten pages like a bird, inspecting where to land.

So mum, the baby's like a visitor who crept into my house one day and sat quietly on this worn armchair. The springs didn't even creak, there wasn't a flutter of breeze. But the visitor has become part of the house, become family.

I remember what you once said to me about your painting. That it didn't come like God. That it seemed to have always been there, waiting for you to turn.

You see? I spent years memorising your soul, and neither of us ever guessed. Memorising how to be both an artist and a mother. In a stumbling sort of way.

Love,
Sally

54 Raymond Crescent
Woy Woy
NSW 2256

Monday, 15 September 1995

Dear Sally,

I got your letters this morning. I'd like to come for a long visit. We could keep the ghosts away together. I don't mind who you sleep with. I wish I'd done the same when I left your father. Could you air the spare room? I'm sure it'll need it. That wasn't a criticism. You know what my asthma's like. But don't do any other tidying up. I want to learn to be messy.

Love,
Mum

ADELE HORIN
The Secret Circle

One of the best things about being the mother of two young boys, now aged six and three, and holding down a paid job, is that I'm part of a secret circle that passes around outrageous stories as our mothers once passed around cakes.

The stories working mothers tell each other can never be told outside the circle. We can't tell our bosses nor our child-free colleagues. They would consider us insufferable whingers, angling for martyrdom. Nor can we tell the mothers who have chosen the at-home option lest they use the stories as ammunition against us.

But within the circle, we relate our sagas until tears roll down our cheeks—tears of sympathy, understanding and hilarity. The stories have two major themes, and we never tire of them: how we got to work on time that

167

morning and what happened the night before.

The story of how working mothers get to the office, factory or shop at nine or earlier each morning is an untold epic. Only Odysseus himself wrestled with so many monsters, fought so many battles, and endured such harassment as the average working mother encounters on her odyssey from bed to desk. If the country were run with the efficiency working mothers bring to their early morning labours, Australia would be an economic tiger, not a kitten.

But it's a secret triumph, which only the inner circle can celebrate. People who roll out of bed with AM on the radio, who *go for a run*, who sip their coffee or nibble their crumpet in peace before jumping on a bus with a favourite novel in hand, have no clue of the three hours' labour a working mother has put in before she gets to work. And she can't tell them. That's her private life, and it's boring and irrelevant to the bosses who favour 7.30 power break-fast meetings; whose children, if they have any, are grown up, or are Someone Else's responsibility.

Odysseus took twenty years to make his trip from the battlefields of Troy to home and that's how long the average working mother feels she's been on the road by the time she arrives in her newly downsized and pressurised workplace. To her, it feels like arriving at a health farm. After all, no one is throwing their muffin at her, throwing up, or throwing a tantrum on the floor.

Few working mothers I know have sex in the morning

any more. But many hang out a load of washing in the dawn light before they go to work. They've covered school books, breastfed babies, and cut school lunches. They've cajoled sleepy children out of bed and force-fed them breakfast. They've strapped masks to the asthmatics and nebulised them. They've dealt with tantrums and sock fetishists, with toddlers who insist on dressing themselves and children who won't get dressed.

They've cleaned up kitchens, bathrooms and bedrooms, and finally themselves before flying out the door, entreating their brood to follow. They've faced down a monster worse than the one-eyed Cyclops—the child who *won't sit in her car seat*. And they've resisted following Odysseus' example. Instead of putting a stake through her, they've used child psychology, even though it's more time-consuming. They've dropped their children at schools, kindergartens and childcare centres, negotiated the peak hour, hunted for all-day parking spaces, caught buses, taxis in emergencies, and hit the desk at opening time.

And that's a good day. Working mothers don't bother to recount the ordinary. It's the variations of the theme they relish during snatched conversations in the canteen queue.

'You won't believe it,' one will whisper to the other. (Oh yes we will!)

'A casserole dish fell on Alex's head this morning and he had to get stitches.'

Or, 'I was driving so fast this morning, I crashed into the back of a Merc.'

Or, 'We'd finally got out of the house and Phoebe vomited all over my blouse.'

'You have to laugh,' we say to each other.

Every time I hear politicians exhorting Australians to work harder, I think of this female underground, these unsung heroes, toiling invisibly in the grey dawn in order to get to work on time. For some women, getting to work is the hardest part of the day. The rest is easy. No tantrum from a boss compares with a two-year-old's; no deadline feels more pressing than the daily deadline of vacating the house.

When I first returned to office work, after my second child, the prospect of a nine o'clock start threw me into a panic. Even before the children, I had never got anywhere by nine o'clock. I like to linger over breakfast, to read the paper, to work late. Journalism has accommodated and accentuated these whims. Few in the business start before ten.

But now I was to do a retraining course for my first stint in radio. It began promptly at nine am. It meant leaving home by 7.45 with a baby and a three-year-old. It seemed like mission impossible. I researched the practicalities as I would a story. I took working mothers to lunch. I badgered them on the telephone. I ruined dinner parties with my interrogations. While the men talked about work, I cajoled the women into telling me how they got to work. I asked intelligent women with double degrees if they showered in the morning or at night; if they ate breakfast before they got dressed or after; at what point did they get the children up; what if the children refused to budge? In a crowded café people shot me funny looks when I grilled a friend about breastfeeding. Did she express milk in the toilet, or in her office, at morning tea or at lunchtime? No detail was too minor.

The secret stories tumbled out. A picture emerged of super-organised women, who finished dinner and started working again. They made up bottles and lunches, they packed bags and briefcases, they laid out every item of their workclothes from earrings to overcoats. They confided handy hints and cautionary tales. Buy your children a dozen pair of socks the same colour. Never buy anything that has to be ironed. They leaned over to whisper the working mother's best-kept secret: *put your children to bed in their dayclothes*. They pointed out common hurdles to getting to the office, and how to straddle them. For example, house keys, car keys, magic buttons, magnetic cards for carpark stations, and magnetic passes for entry to the high-tech office must always be kept in one place.

Bit by bit, I pieced together the remarkable story of how mothers get to work on time. It helps if you are by nature a cheerful early riser, have one child, or older children, have a partner who shares the morning rigours, live close to work and childcare, or have a nanny. It helps if you work only three or four days a week.

But is it worth it, I asked them? Why subject yourself to such pressure? They need the money, they love the work, maternity leave is too short, they're bored witless at home, they're scared they won't get back into the workforce if they take too many years off. Old hands said the routine got easier with practice. You might be worn out, they said, but the kids thrived with good childcare. They turned out normal, affectionate, happy, and by the time the school years rolled round, were independent, gregarious and never questioned having a working mum. As the kids got older, the women told me, they did more for themselves. You had more time, you got to shower in the mornings again . . . And also you were part of a secret sisterhood who told each other outrageous stories.

Finally the dawn rose (literally) on my new life. Like a colonel I rounded up the troops and the supplies. Everything went to plan. My older son, bless his heart, was thrilled to be one of the first at childcare. And I could not believe it. I was the first at the retraining room. The young ones, the childfree ones, stumbled in at 9.15. Four years earlier, that would have been me.

Working mothers experience the rest of the day differently, too, especially the lunch hour. Working mothers don't usually *do* lunch. And if they occasionally give in to temptation, they usually regret it. For a working mother, lunch is like an extra-marital affair—two parts pleasure, eight parts guilt. As soon as it's over, she's asking herself if it was worth it. Twenty-five dollars for a snippet of gossip and a chicken breast.

Working mothers are lousy lunch dates. It's not that they cut up your steak or wipe the cappuccino froth off your upper lip. It's just that they're tense. They look at their watch a lot. They hassle the waiter. It's harder, granted, for everyone to do lunch the way they used to before the hard-edged nineties. But it's still easier for men. It's unprofessional for a professional man to be seen leaving the office before six or seven. But most working mothers have to leave their jobs around five. Usually they are the first to sneak out the door, cursing the fetish for open-plan offices that give bosses a panoramic view of comings and goings. But they have to pick up children from childcare centres and nannies and after-school care.

There aren't enough hours in the work day for most busy professional women, without losing an hour or more to lunch. They have long since abandoned past lunchtime pleasures such as stretching their legs, clearing their heads, buying pantyhose, paying the car registration. And eating in a relaxed and convivial manner in a restaurant.

Working mothers are the face of the future, working not longer, but harder and smarter. You can always get them on the phone between one and two. They're clearing their in-tray, drafting a letter, polishing a report. And that's when they tell each other stories, in fifteen-minute bites, huddling over yoghurts and salad rolls at each others' desks.

'I went to lunch yesterday,' one will confess, 'with so-and-so.' (A notorious luncher.)

Oh yes, we know. We have all fallen into temptation.

'He ordered an entrée,' she'll say in horrified tones. 'He ordered a bottle of wine. I felt I couldn't leave.'

We can see the lunch stretching out, we envisage the chaos that awaits her at the other end of the day—the scramble to finish a story on time, the race to beat the twenty-dollar fine at the after-school centre for five minutes' lateness.

'Next time invite another man to go with you,' we advise. 'He'll be able to stay and finish the wine.'

We tell each other, 'You've got to laugh.'

We thought our social life, our gossip quotient would expand when we returned to work. Often we hardly knew a soul in the street. Our real community was the office. And back in the office, our network shrinks to the phone and the fax. And each other.

By 4.45 most working mothers have a demonic look in their eye. They are working to beat the clock. Working mothers never tell each other stories in the last half hour of the day. They bitterly resent the others who initiate friendly but useless conversations. Working mothers know the value of ten minutes. They know how much can be achieved in five. The only conversations they start up are with their husbands, and only in an emergency when they must negotiate a change of schedule. Say a union meeting has been called for five and a working mother really wants to go. Or say it's Christmas time, and she's been invited to a cocktail party.

A cocktail party? For working mothers the cocktail hour is the arsenic hour. Working mothers usually bypass a large slice of community life—yoga, Politics in the Pub, book launchings, committee meetings—anything, in short, that starts at 5.30 and ends a couple of hours later. It's an embarrassment to have to fill out a form that asks about 'other interests', and 'membership of professional associations ... etc'. How dull it sounds to admit to no other interests but work and family and to no associations but the secret circle, which doesn't count.

Attending a meeting, giving a public talk, any regular commitments that take them away from quality time with the children, feel as sinful as an affair. And that's one story you never hear in the secret circle. Working mothers don't have time for affairs.

But say a working mother wants to break out, feel like a citizen again, part of the political process, a contributor to public life. And the meeting or the event is naturally in the two-hour time slot that for others is a convenient wedge between day and night-time activities. The working mother must negotiate with her partner. Negotiation is what working couples must master or die. Their marriage resembles less a union of lovers than a union of workers. They are the perfect enterprise bargaining unit. 'If you pick up Alex tonight, I'll pick up the take-away'; 'Can you pick up the take-away and I'll take Phoebe to the doctor?'; 'If I can go to the meeting tonight, I'll do the shopping on Saturday and you can go into the office'.

Marriage was once called a battleground. But a working mother's marriage looks more like an industrial relations minefield. The secret circle of working mothers exchanges progress reports on the key issues of enterprise bargaining— time management ('the kids were in bed by 8.30!'), productivity (the ten-minute stir-fry recipe), and demarcation disputes ('he never hears the baby cry'). It rejoices in good news stories about teamwork and multi-skilling on the home front ('John does the morning shift, I do the night shift').

Now I'd be lying if I said it doesn't get me down sometimes—the search for the formula for a balanced life. A man, a job and kids ought to guarantee me a terrific life. But a lot of the time as I rush hither and thither I feel the terrific life is elusive. My jawline is too tense. My fuse too short.

Yet I, like the friends in my secret circle of working mothers, could not go back to the exclusively private, homebound lives of our mothers' generation. Boredom and lack of self-esteem sent many mothers, mine included, into the workforce to save themselves. Being housewives guaranteed neither marriages of depth and intimacy, nor grateful children. So we working mothers grapple with getting the parts right, wonder whether our lives of negotiation and deadlines amount to happiness; whether having it all is just too much.

But as I look at my amazing children, growing up competent and delightful, maybe even because of their parents' crazy lifestyle, I for one think this might be the best of times. Working mothers of young children have always existed. But now there is a critical mass of us, a circle of women to confide in, laugh and cry with, who know exactly what it's like.

GABRIELLE CAREY

Prenatal Depression, Postmodern World

The day after I gave birth to my first child I sat breastfeeding on my sunny verandah in Veracruz, Mexico, convinced that up until that moment my entire life had been a ridiculous waste of time. I cursed myself for having left such a wonderful event so late, and silently calculated how many more children I could fit into what was left of my childbearing lifetime. There just didn't seem to be anything else to do that could possibly feel as fulfilling. It was like falling madly in love. Except I knew that mother love would be a lot more lasting than romantic love.

Whenever I describe these feelings to people I watch them as their expressions gradually tighten, their eyes diminishing to slits, their minds transparently suspicious. It sounds too much like an ecstatic Christian conversion

179

to be true. What about the pain, they're thinking, that excruciating pain of labour we've all heard so much about?

So I then have to confess to my perfect textbook birth. Yes there was pain but it didn't seem to me, for the most part, unbearable. Even the excruciating moments, when the head was squeezing out and I screamed as I felt myself being literally stretched beyond endurance. There was something different about the pain. It was pain with meaning. Yes, I suffered. But it was an exquisite sort of suffering which yielded an exquisite beauty—my baby.

A few days after the birth I took the baby out for a walk. I think I wanted to show her off more than anything. I remember how annoyed I felt when I was chastised by the other women in the village for having left the house before the traditional forty days' confinement expired. A silly, oppressive tradition, I thought. But for women who work such long, arduous hours—and most women in third world villages rise long before dawn and are relieved of duties late in the evening only if their husbands and children make no demands during the night—the month after the birth of a baby and the attention they get from visitors must be the closest thing to a holiday they ever experience. To remove the forty-day confinement rule would be disastrous. I could afford to go for a leisurely stroll a few days after my baby was born because I would have plenty of other time to rest, during and after the forty days. But at the time I thought they had no right to tell me when I was allowed to leave my own home with my own baby.

There were other postnatal rules in the village that also annoyed me, such as the belief that babies had to be carried horizontally at all times. Whenever I walked the streets with my baby over my shoulder I was warned that if I persisted with this position my daughter would certainly suffer from green diarrhoea. I was given this advice so often I eventually ignored my own self-imposed rule not to preach Western beliefs and explained earnestly to these women why modern medicine had shown that there was no relation whatsoever between diarrhoea and the way in which an infant was carried. They all shook their heads in despair at my ignorance. Even my husband, quite educated by village standards, was caught between the strength of his traditional beliefs and the strength of my 'rational' arguments. To make things worse, soon after, Brigid actually *did* suffer from greenish diarrhoea. Of course I knew the cause had to lie elsewhere but there was no use insisting. As far as my opponents were concerned they'd been proven right.

There were many nice things too, however, about Mexican beliefs regarding newborn babies. It was a custom, for example, that before visitors entered the house to view the newborn baby, they always waited outside on the patio just in case they were carrying 'bad air'. This made sense to me. When a baby is born it seems so pure and so vulnerable that the world outside its immediate

181

vicinity feels all the more polluted and poisonous. It's natural to want to create a little area of safety around the angelic innocence of a newborn. As a way of ensuring that a child remains unharmed from any wayward bad influence that might penetrate this little area, there was a tradition in the village known as 'cleaning' the baby. This meant no more than taking a handful of fresh leaves from a special cleansing herb and brushing them over the child while saying a prayer. But it was quite a pleasant, reassuring ritual.

Another practice among the village mothers was to massage babies in order to 'release tension'. It's hard to imagine how babies could suffer from tension but my daughter obviously enjoyed her massages. In fact, she positively seemed to revel in the sensuality of skin against skin. Babies in Mexico don't have separate rooms and separate cots which meant that, by sleeping with Brigid, I became even more aware of her intense sensuality, to the point where I came close to being unnerved by the almost sexual nature of our closeness. While breastfeeding she seemed to purr with contentment and I knew it wasn't just the satisfaction of appetite. Long after she was weaned, she still liked to put her little hand down my bra and feel the comfort of warm, bulky flesh and nipple. This was frowned upon by some as a sign of gross insecurity or even mild perversion but by the age of two she had naturally grown out of her attachment to the breast. If she hadn't, I'm sure people would have been encouraging me to take her to a child psychologist. To some the thought of infantile sensuality is incomprehensible; to others, positively repulsive.

In some ways, having a baby in Mexico was difficult. In the village there were no baby health centres, and few reliable doctors. The water supply was contaminated with amoebas. The milk was unpasteurised and unhomogenised. Nappies had to be laboriously handwashed. The roads were cobbled or unpaved, making it impossible to push a stroller even if you could afford one. And the reality of babies dying from dehydration caused by diarrhoea was always present.

And yet, in another sense, having a baby in Mexico was actually much easier than having a baby in Australia simply because the attitude to mothers and mothering is so different. In Mexico being pregnant isn't seen as something that automatically diminishes your life—socially, culturally and economically. Babies are always welcome, despite the poverty. In fact, there was a saying in the village that when a baby came into the world it always brought its own sandwich under its arm. That is, a baby cost nothing, or very little, in terms of food, the most important and pressing need in any third world village.

About my first pregnancy I remember three things: cooking, sewing and daydreaming. I was constantly hungry so I was constantly preparing food. I had very little money so I sewed my own maternity dresses and baby clothes. And while I cooked and sewed I daydreamed about the baby. Neither my husband nor I had a secure income or any potential for one. The thought of future schooling or childcare never crossed my mind. Neither did it occur to me that having a baby might permanently damage my career. Practicalities just didn't enter into it. The whole experience seemed like a wonderful adventure.

Now, seven years later, in a different country and a different relationship, I am expecting my second child. Instead of daydreaming I worry—about my career, about childcare and about my son or daughter's future education. I also worry that the pain of labour will seem much, much worse. By living a less privileged lifestyle in Mexico—by that I mean I had no modern amenities such as washing machines, cars, kitchen appliances—my threshold for suffering or my ability for just 'putting up' with things rose considerably. Now that I've been back in the lucky country for several years I feel that the toughness I developed in Mexico has been gradually eroded by 'the good life' and I am left to contend with that paradox of the first world: the more we have available for alleviating suffering, the more sensitive to suffering we become. For that reason, and because it's far cheaper, I've decided on a birth centre instead of a home delivery. But it's not as simple as it sounds.

'Hello? Yes. My name is ... I'm calling from Sydney ... I'm coming to Canberra for six months and during that time I'm having a baby ... would Doctor Stevens be available as a sharecare doctor for the birth centre?'

This is the fifth time I've been through this spiel. None of the busy male doctors specialising in obstetrics can fit me into their tight schedules. I suppose it must be very difficult for them on such minimal salaries. They only earn $140 an hour to deliver a baby. Midwives earn $15.76.

'When are you expecting?' the polite secretary asks.

'October.'

'Oh no, sorry. There's no space left in October.'

I am getting so sick of hearing that. It sounds like I'm being told I'm simply not allowed to have a baby in October. It's too inconvenient for the doctors. I'll just have to wait.

'Well I don't actually *need* a doctor,' I say haughtily. 'I've already had a baby at home with a midwife *without* a doctor. It's just one of the requirements of the birth centre. I need his okay so I can go there.'

I'm infuriated. Why on earth do I need some anonymous man's permission to have a baby?

'Well I'm sorry. We just can't fit you in.'

I slam down the phone. I know I shouldn't be blaming the secretary but I can't help it. With my first baby in Mexico, my ante-natal consultations consisted of two casual visits to our house by a doctor friend. And he didn't tell me anything I didn't already know. In Australia the medical profession seems to want you to think that

185

you couldn't possibly do it without them. Neither could you do it without blood tests, urine tests, internal examinations, ultrasounds and then, when you get to the age of thirty-six, more blood tests for Downs syndrome, amniocentesis and a full GTT.

Just as we've medicalised death and taken it out of the hands of family and friends and communities, so have we medicalised birth, to the point where the hospital, the institution I hate most after prison, is the only place that responds clearly to the call of my pregnancy.

I don't mean to say that there aren't many things to appreciate about the Australian health system. The main reason I decided to have a home birth with my first baby was because the public hospitals in Mexico were so intolerable. But it was also because, in a Mexican village, hospitals aren't seen as all that relevant to pregnancy. Most women have their babies delivered at home with only a midwife attending. It is women's business and women are in control. Admittedly, when problem births occur, this can mean disastrous consequences. I was once told about a breech birth attended by a traditional midwife in a remote village where the only way of extracting the infant was to sever its limbs first. But these incidents are rare. It is assumed that most women will have normal deliveries of normal babies, and most do.

In comparison, in Australia, I am told I *must* have ante-natal care from a hospital; and while waiting the mandatory two hours for my first consultation in the King

George ante-natal clinic, I can't help getting the impression that my pregnancy is out of my control, beyond my capacity to handle and necessarily the responsibility of someone wiser, more educated and, more often than not, male. The fact that most women, with emotional support and encouragement, are capable of having babies all on their own doesn't seem to be reflected in medical practice at all. As I sit in the queue, women all around me wait nervously to be processed through the system, obviously intimidated yet eager to be told, by a male stranger, exactly what to do about this uncomfortable state in which they've found themselves.

When my number is finally called (no, I'm not exaggerating—we are called by *number*, not by name) I am shunted from weighing station to urine sampling, from stomach-prodding doctors to ultrasound, and then lastly to a little room with one woman who does nothing all day but stick syringes in strangers' veins. It is only after my third enquiry and the fourth vial has been extracted that I am finally told what my blood is being tested for.

Before leaving I am given a date to return for my GTT test.

'What is a GTT anyway?' I ask the nurse, because it is obvious I'm not going to be told.

'A Glucose Tolerance Test.' She hands me a sheet of paper, presumably as explanation. In fact, it has no explanation at all, only a list of instructions to those who are to undergo a GTT. It means another morning at the hospital, another needle in the vein. And I can tell by the look in the nurse's eyes that it is a modern torture experience.

'What if I don't want it?' I ask. She looks up at me, momentarily speechless. Obviously no one has ever asked this question before.

On the way home from the hospital I look at the instructions for the GTT. It tells me that it will take two to three hours and that the results will be known within twenty-four hours. It also tells me that for three days before the test I have to start a high carbohydrate diet, eating *at least* six slices of bread, one serving of breakfast cereal, two potatoes, three servings of vegetables, three servings of fruit, two biscuits and one scone every day. No wonder they don't do this in Mexico, I think. But it still doesn't explain what the test is looking for or what a 'problem' result might mean. And I assume that there are very few women demanding explanations. Just like the village women who submit themselves unquestioningly to *curanderas* who claim to be performing magic acts of healing, so most first world women submit themselves to doctors with little effort at finding out what the purpose of these modern day rituals actually are.

On my next visit to the hospital I drop into the maternity information centre. Despite my disillusion with the Australian health system I am determined to take advantage of the services available to pregnant women which hadn't been available in Mexico and which I had longed for in my first pregnancy. Or at least thought I had. A matronly woman gives me numerous pamphlets on diet, health and breastfeeding as well as a list of free fitness classes for pregnant women. I can choose from stretching exercises, yoga or aerobics.

In a Mexican village there are no such thing as fitness classes—whether you're pregnant or not—and even if there were, no woman would have the time or energy to go to them. Besides, when you're picking coffee eight to ten hours a day, you're probably far fitter than even the most dedicated Australian gym junkie. Underweight is always a much bigger problem than overweight.

At twelve weeks I enrol in the Friday morning exercise class. I'm still not 'showing', thank God, though my elevation to extra-support Double D cup is showy enough. As I stretch and strain I look around and to my relief, not one woman is proportioned in the way we're told we ought to be, in the way the fashion magazines would have us. Instead, we all have bits sticking out where they shouldn't be, bursting out from all sorts of odd places as we puff and pant in a pathetic attempt at holding in our ever-slackening seams.

'Tummy in! Bottom tucked under!' our instructor repeats over and over. 'That's it! Good girls!'

Why are we always girls and never women? Even at thirty-six?

'Now girls, time for our pelvic floor exercises. Tighten

the buttocks. Pull up the muscles around the vagina and the anus. Hold and relax. Now again. Pull up. Hold and relax. This is a most important exercise. During pregnancy and labour a lot of damage can be done to the pelvic floor. The muscles sag and become slack. The pressure on the uterus means you'll sometimes find you wet yourself. Some women can suffer incontinence during pregnancy and if you're not careful it may continue after the baby is born. Slackening of the vaginal muscles can also mean loss of sensation and enjoyment of sex. So we must all do our pelvic exercises at least ten times a day. Pull up and relax. Up and relax.'

As I lie on the floor along with a dozen other women, pulling and relaxing invisible, internal muscles, I realise that although I do appreciate these free services and all this information, I'm really not sure if I have the time or energy to worry about my pelvic floor as well as everything else. I've already been informed at my first ante-natal visit that I have to worry about my caffeine and alcohol intake and that the two Irish coffees I indulged in when I was six weeks pregnant could well cause foetal brain damage. I've also been told that I should worry about my low iron levels. That I should eat plenty of liver but avoid pâté (to me, the only edible source of liver), because it can cause lis- teriosis which can lead to a stillborn. As can smoked salmon and camembert cheese, my two favourite deli- cacies. I've also been informed that my two cats can cause foetal damage if I come into contact with their excrement. And that, according to the ultrasound, the baby is too small.

And that is just what the hospital has told me to worry about.

Apart from that, there are the things other people suggest that I *should* worry about. Like money. I don't have a proper job with maternity leave. As a freelance writer I barely eke out an existence. The first well-paying job I've ever had starts when I am five months pregnant. How will I cope? asks my sister-in-law. Is there childcare available at the university? Perhaps I should put the baby's name down now on one of those mile-long waiting lists for day care. Will I be able to express enough milk to leave behind when I go to work? Should I invest in an electric breast pump? Will the baby take a bottle? And now, on top of all this, it seems that I will soon be left in a state of middle-aged incontinence due to the imminent collapse of my pelvic floor.

I glance up from my stretching exercises and catch an unwanted glimpse of myself in the wall-length mirror of the hospital exercise room, reminding me of another niggling but persistent worry: will my breasts ever again return to their semi-normal 34C?

As I contemplate my bulbous body stretching to the rhythm of Madonna's 'Like a Virgin', I begin to understand why people look at me with a mixture of pity and revulsion when I announce 'my condition'.

'Was it intended?' is the usual response, implying that it couldn't have been otherwise than unintended.

'Oh you *are* going to be busy!' is another. Meaning: My God, how will you possibly manage?

And then there is my most unfavourite comment of all that keeps resounding in my head: 'Oh you really *do* like to make things hard for yourself, don't you Gabrielle?'

Do I? Is that really my motive? Is bearing children just my perverse way of seeking suffering? A subconscious masochistic impulse? Maybe there's something seriously wrong with me. Perhaps I should see a psychotherapist after all.

Of course this last suggestion comes from a childless woman who simply cannot imagine why anyone would complicate their already complex life with babies.

'Children just don't fit into my lifestyle,' she says nonchalantly, as if there are other people whose lifestyles are tailor-made to sleeplessness and dirty nappies.

When the exercise class ends I look around at the other women, as though it were the conclusion of a clandestine meeting, a secret underground sect of single-minded recalcitrants, ignorant of ZPG, thoughtlessly pushing the world closer to ecological disaster by insisting on exercising their fertility. I detect—or is it just my imagination?—that stolen look of shared guilt, as the rounded figures farewell their fellow sisters in crime, careful now to have dressed in a manner that disguises their real identity, giving each other final gestures of solidarity to help brave the disapproval of the outside world until the next meeting.

I am on the verge of that unenviable age of thirty-seven, (and I *still* haven't been to Paris). Most women of my age will know at least one other woman who has spent the last decade or so weighing up the pros and cons of having children or not having children, swinging in indecision year after year until finally it's too late. These women apply rational, intelligent thought to a problem which, they believe, *must* have a rational, intelligent solution. Discussing this 'problem' with an internationally known writer at a literary festival recently, I was interested to note that most important to the debate was what children cost, not in terms of money, but in terms of time. It seemed like a particularly peculiar attitude coming from a writer. Very few novels 'earn back' the time and effort invested in them. You write them simply because you must. To be a writer, you can't afford to apply the rules of investment and return. And yet this attitude of trying to surmise whether the harvest will be worth the sowing was automatically applied to children.

'I suppose you'd have to give up about ... oh ... fifty per cent of your time,' I said.

'Fifty per cent?' came the shocked response. That would mean less books written, less film deals, less travel. The cost was obviously too high.

In a sense it's as though economic rationalism—or some

warped branch of it—is being applied to mothering and motherhood. But just as there are some products which will never find a profitable place for themselves in the 'market'—such as poetry for example—having babies can never 'pay off', at least not in contemporary first world culture. In our society our children will not support us when we grow old or help us pick coffee in the fields from the age of five, as they do in Mexico. So rationally speaking, I suppose the pain, the cost, the time involved in having children really is too high. But the same could be said about love. Or life.

The fact that the fear of having children—how they will change, diminish, limit our lives—appears to be the reason behind many people's decisions to stay childless, seems to me to be a symptom of an even deeper fear of life itself. Having children means they would become too *involved*. This is, undeniably, a well-founded fear. Once you're a mother you do become permanently and inextricably involved. Your sense of self, so precious in a society where religion has been largely replaced with the philosophy of individualism, is indefinitely blurred. From the moment the baby is born, whatever you feel will be reflected in her and whatever she feels will be reflected in you. Most mothers have experienced the feeling of the milk 'coming down' when they are physically nowhere near the baby, signalling that the baby wants to feed. Or the sensation of a baby's crying causing breasts to leak. Even now, if I am lying awake at night, worried about something, my daughter will often wake up with a nightmare, often directly related to whatever I'm worried about at that moment, as though my fears and anxieties have been magically transmitted to her in the next room. When she recounts her bad dream to me, sometimes her subconscious has understood my problem better than I. And occasionally, she will inadvertently provide me with an insight that I would never have arrived at on my own, no matter how much midnight analysing and rationalising I applied.

Remarking recently on aspects of contemporary morality, the cartoonist Michael Leunig said that he thought a lot of modern problems came from the fact that we have to do everything at speed. 'We have to love our children *at speed*,' he said.

The reason we have to do everything at speed is because we're so busy. All of us are guilty of claiming that we simply have 'no time'. Our perception that we have 'no time', says Canadian anthropologist Margaret Visser, 'is one of the distinctive marks of modern Western culture . . . We have "no time" apparently because modern life offers so many pleasures, so many choices, that we cannot resist trying enough of them to "use up" all the time we have been allotted.'

In other words, the more things we have, the less time we have to enjoy them. The more our so-called standard of living increases, the harder it is to enjoy.

Now that I live in the lucky country, I no longer have

the leisure to embroider ladybirds on bibs as I did for my first baby. I no longer spend hours just contemplating different names and their meanings. I'm in too much of a hurry. Even when I try to take time off to visualise the baby, all my other concerns come crashing into the picture and block it out. I can't even dream about the baby. I'm just *too busy*.

This is why I sometimes reflect nostalgically on my lifestyle in Mexico, despite the poverty. I think of the slow plodding pace of a subsistence village, of the simplicity of everyone's wants and needs. Of the leisure of relaxing in a phoneless, faxless environment. From my privileged yet prenatally depressed existence, I look back fondly on my first pregnancy when I had nothing more urgent to do than sew and cook.

So why can't I just give up those things that are stopping me from sitting around embroidering babies' clothes? Why can't I forget about career-building, about house improvements and earning enough money for my daughter's dance lessons? Why can't I just return to the Mexican lifestyle? If it was so good over there, why did I ever come back? Silly as it may sound, my decision to repatriate was triggered by one small thing: worms.

In Mexico my daughter was nicknamed *Gordita*, which means Little Fattie (a compliment there, not an insult)— and she was indeed quite weighty compared to the other village children. By Australian standards however (as I was later informed by a well-meaning baby health care sister), she was vastly underweight. The reason for this was intestinal worms. Not the kind of worms we have in Australia. These were an altogether nastier, more insidious variety of worms which contribute to general malnutrition and quite often death in children in so-called underdeveloped countries. When I realised that Brigid, at eighteen months, had worms, I treated her with medicine and was told by the doctor that this powerful elixir would cause the parasites to be 'expelled'. The next morning when I changed Brigid's nappy I found a seething nest of milk-white worms, the like of which I had only ever seen in horror movies. My first response was to call my mother. My second was an intense desire to return to Australia.

It wasn't just the hideous encounter with a squirming clump of worms the size of a cricket ball that made me want to return to the safe, if sterile, Australian lifestyle; it was the realisation that Brigid had no choice but to co-exist indefinitely with these creatures if she were to remain in Mexico. Unless I segregated her from the other children in the street—who suffered constantly from a whole range of intestinal parasites—she would only ever stay uninfected for a few days at a time. I tried handing out medicine the length and breadth of the neighbourhood and it worked for a couple of days. But as soon as the children went back to playing with the piglets kept behind the house for fattening, as soon as they returned to defecating where there were no latrines, to sharing food without washing their hands, the tiny eggs that triggered the cycle of worm infestation once again found nice warm breeding grounds in the intestines of innocent, underfed children.

Maybe it was the puritan in me that overreacted to the parasites which are so common in many parts of the world. Most of the other kids survived. Brigid would have too. Underweight she might always have been and under normal height, but there would have been no other long-term effects. Cowardly as I now think it was, from that moment on, I could no longer cope with the hardships of third world existence.

Of course, in many ways I have only exchanged one set of hardships for another. I am not at all sure that Brigid is happier or better off in the first world than the third. Infested with worms the Mexican children might have been, but at least there *were* children in the neighbourhood. In the street where I now live there are no children at all, with or without worms. Have I opted for cold isolated cleanliness instead of a warm community grubbiness? Can we ever know 'what's best' for our children? Or ourselves for that matter? Despite our education, our intelligence, our twenty-first century technology, I very much doubt it. No matter how much well-educated analysis we indulge in, life is not (thank God) just another problem to which we, with our ever-increasing knowledge, will eventually find a solution. It is a gift to be experienced, suffered and enjoyed.

So it is with children.

PAT MAMAJUN TORRES
Mowangka's Birth:
a promise of a new life

It was a sweltering kind of day when Mowangka was born. The hustle and bustle of family Christmas parties and the usual gift-giving rituals were over, and the quiet town of Rubibi had returned to its free and easy lifestyle.

She was born in the early hours of the morning when most of the people in the town were fast asleep. Only the midwife was there to welcome her into the world as the local doctor had gone home an hour ago, convinced that the labour would take hours and hours. But Mowangka was not going to do what the doctor wanted: she had made up her own mind when it was time for her to be born.

Her own father had also gone home; she was not going to wait for him either. Her mother had been lying there quietly, trying to rest for the hard labour she knew was going to happen sometime that night.

As she rested, concentrating on positive thoughts, Mowangka's mother reflected back to the first time that she instinctively knew that something very special was going to happen in her life in the coming months ahead.

It was one day after the Kimberley wet season, when her family had gone to spend the weekend with her mother's brother's family of in-laws who lived at Fitzroy Crossing. She remembered how the whole family had loaded up their belongings into the four-wheel drive and bumped their way along the rough river roads and the washaways on the eroded and flat river plains, to the junction in the off-shoot of the Fitzroy River, known to the local people as Dawadiya.

The landscape of Dawadiya was spectacular. There were beautifully polished smooth river stones that varied in size from the small man-made cutting tools of hunters in days gone by, to the boulders that lined the river bank. The roughness of the gravelly river sand could be heard crunching under tender feet as you walked searching along the cool river banks for gagarru, the freshwater mussel. On the sides of the river banks were tall silent paperbark trees that stood like watchful guardians with outstretched arms of olive green foliage; their branches whispered in the cool afternoon breeze, telling all who cared to listen of the secrets of days now gone.

The clean sweet smell of the riverside was sometimes

masked by the sickly nectar of the creamy paperbark blossoms that attracted the constant attention of the noisy honeyeaters. The blood red, lantern-like flowers of majala, the freshwater mangrove, hung suspended in thin but strong elongated stems that danced in the breeze travelling through the branches of the river trees.

The newly fallen leaves felt smooth, cool and damp under your feet as you wound your way along the steep banks looking for a safe way to get down to the shallow waters. The river beckoned with each glint of sun that reached its rays through the dense foliage.

Mowangka's mother, Banaga, remembered looking towards the far bank and catching a glimpse of a number of gwaniya, or freshwater crocodiles, floating just below the water's surface. Only the tips of their long reptilian snouts and their beady ever-watchful eyes protruded through the surface of the still water.

Banaga had called to her husband and, pointing her fingers, showed him the crocodiles on the far bank. Burungu, her husband, became excited and ran back to the car to get his rifle, while Banaga made her way carefully towards the far right-hand bank to look for gagarru, the freshwater mussel.

So busy looking for the gagarru, Banaga forgot for a minute that her husband had gone to fetch his gun, until all of a sudden she heard the loud crack of a rifle shot which passed close by. She jumped at the piercing noise, and immediately looked in the direction of the sound to see her husband on the opposite river bank shooting his .22 rifle at the crocodiles.

Then suddenly one well-aimed bullet hit the leathery head of a metre-long crocodile, sending the creature leaping high into the air above the water, like a barramundi caught at last at the end of a fishing line. The crocodile dived deep into the emerald waters of the river, then immediately surfaced. Its wounded body began to float towards Banaga, who was now walking near the junction of two small riverlets, towards the place called Dawadiya.

Burungu had called out to his wife and told her to grab hold of the crocodile as it writhed in its final death throes and continued to float towards her. Banaga obeyed him, quickly wading out to the dying crocodile. Without fear, she firmly grasped it in both hands then turned to carry it to shore; her husband was already rushing around collecting the dry wood needed to make a fire large enough to cook his catch.

As Banaga carried the crocodile up the bank, the old people and all the children, attracted by the commotion, had rushed around her, very excited because the freshwater crocodile had died so easily, floating up quickly after being shot directly towards Banaga. They had all begun to talk excitedly, saying that it was something special for a crocodile to do that. Normally a wounded crocodile would dive straight into his watery home. It would take hours for the water to seep into the wounds in his skin, and then he would begin to die slowly, inside his own underground tunnel. This event was considered to be really unusual, something spiritual, and extraordinary; and later Banaga found out just what was so special about this incident.

Some months after, Banaga had discovered that she was expecting another child, and went to tell her uncle's in-laws about the great news. They had become excited all over again, and responded by saying that her new baby must surely have the spirit of that gwaniya, the freshwater crocodile that her husband had shot on the river bank at Dawadiya junction. This meant that the child's special symbol would be Gwaniya, and that the child's bush name in the riverside should be Dawadiya. Whenever the child would visit her relations in the riverside communities, she would be able to talk about her connections to Dawadiya and the freshwater crocodile. This would be important to her, as it would automatically give her social connections with the kinship systems and the people of that region. And for as long as she lived in the saltwater environment, she would refer to her connections with the black-lipped oyster Dreaming, and her Yawuru bush name, Mowangka, would be used.

These interchanging connections to names, places and dreamings would always provide her with a cultural context appropriate for her situation. They would ensure that she could move across and within cultural boundaries, and always be able to fit in and participate as a member of that group.

A sharp pain in her side brought Banaga's mind back to the present, and as the birth pains grew more intense and more regular, Banaga realised it would not be long before she would look on the face of her newborn child, the child that was to have Gwaniya as one of its special spiritual symbols.

This was Banaga's second child to her husband. The previous birth was of a son, Yunimidi. A son. How different it had been then. They had been living together for just on six months, were head over heels in love, and had decided to get married. She had fallen pregnant during the first week of the honeymoon. It had all been wonderful—a new baby, a new home and car, all in the first year of their marriage. Everything seemed perfect.

He had been there, at the birth of his son, even though it was not the usual practice for their people to allow men to witness the birth; it was still considered traditional women's business.

Now the imminent birth, together with the recent words of her husband convincing her that he would change for her and the children's sake, had given her a sense of new beginnings. She hoped for a change towards a good and happy life.

Banaga laboured strong but she felt relaxed. When it came, the moment of birth was quiet and peaceful after the great urges to push the baby were over. Her youthful body was able to withstand the pain and this capacity was proud testimony to her being a survivor of other traumas suffered in recent times.

It was early, before dawn. Mowangka's mother gazed lovingly at her beautiful daughter. The baby's skin was a golden-brown with flushed rosy cheeks framed by a dark mass of wavy, sticking-up hair. Mowangka was like a fragile porcelain doll: pretty, petite, vulnerable. Her tiny chubby hands were clenched tight in fists and as her mother watched she stuck one thumb between her pouting lips. Banaga gently removed the thumb from the baby's mouth and replaced it with one of her full brown nipples. The baby drank greedily, sucking up the colostrum and milk that was already filling in her mother's breast.

As Banaga gazed at her beautiful daughter she was reminded of her husband's cruel words after the birth. Banaga had felt great pain in her heart when she heard the rejection of his child. She was anguished to hear the words denying his fatherhood. They had cut deeply into her already battered and bruised mind, and sent shivers of fear into her deepest self. Banaga had always been faithful to her husband. Now his accusation that she was with another man while married to him began to darken the light in her soul, and bring into question the love she'd always had for her husband.

His words of denial were tearing away at her feelings. Who was this immature and insecure man who called himself her husband? Where, she wondered, were all his doubts coming from?

Mowangka's father arrived early, shortly after the sun had

risen, demanding to inspect the baby and making sly comments that he didn't think the child resembled him in any way, and generally continuing his usual verbal abuse. His words continued to tear the love for him that she had right out of her heart, and instead, Banaga began to feel a certain numbness that froze the strings of her heart and clouded the light in her soul.

Banaga kept on biting her lips until a small trickle of blood ran down to her chin. She did this to stop herself from answering his accusations, to prevent herself from being pulled into this game of make-believe that didn't stop and seemed to have no known rules. He constantly did this, flinging made-up situations in her face and demanding to know why she did this or that. But the stories were so far from the truth that his words left her speechless, literally. Under these conditions Banaga tried to keep her cool and to remind herself that he was six years younger than she. He didn't have the same level of education. Maybe be needed some time to grow up and understand what it really meant to be a husband and a father.

Banaga remembered how she had tried constantly to show him that she loved him despite his insecurities, and she had hoped that one day he would begin to love her and the children in return. This was why she had gone back to him, even though he had treated her so very badly. With love in her heart and hope in her mind she carried out her duty for the children, to try and make it once again for their sake.

But as she tried to put the thoughts of her husband's previous actions to the back of her mind, the pain remained. The memory of how he had knocked her around in their own home was one that would take many years to heal.

He spoke, almost snarling in anger.

'She looks more like you than me! My other daughter to that woman in Barula looks like me, but not this one!'

Banaga was hurt by the stupid insensitivity of his words, but she responded defensively.

'Well, of course she's gotta look like me, I'm her mother aren't I? And you're her father. If you don't believe it you can just get out of here right now 'cause I've had enough of this nonsense and your ridiculous accusations that don't have any truth in them. Why don't you just go—go away now, I've had enough!'

The unexpected outburst made Burungu quiet all of a sudden, and he did stop his ramblings. Feeling, no doubt, the tension of the moment, and hearing the loud noises, the baby moved restlessly. She gazed upwards and looked deep into her mother's eyes as if trying to give her some kind of comfort and strength.

'All right then,' said Burungu, 'when are you goin' to get out of here?'

'I suppose when the doctors say I can go home.' Her voice was soft again.

'I'll be back later to pick you up.' And he strode out of the room still in a huff.

When Burungu left them the cold and antiseptic room returned to its previous air of quiet and calm. Mother and daughter continued to gaze with love and wonder at each other, warming themselves by the strength of their feelings. One of the baby's chubby hands was held out to be grasped by her mother, while the other searched for something else to clasp onto until it found her mother's long brown hair. As they gazed into each other's eyes there seemed to be a moment of understanding: at least they had each other. The love that flowed between them now would blossom and grow to get them through the days of conflict that lay ahead.

Mowangka

A child born, not dark, not fair, but a golden brown,
born with hair so dark, now turned to a coppery tone,
eyes that shine wide and oval-shaped round,
my child Mowangka, she born from Yawuru ground.

Her Dreaming is the black-lipped oyster
that sits firmly on the rock, lap lapped by the salt water.

Mowangka, a spirit-child from my Yawuru Dreaming,
came to me,
her birth place not far from the legendary tracks down near
    Minyirr,
or Gantheaume Point,
beside the sea.

Mowangka little oyster girl,
a Yawuru/Jabirr-Jabirr child
with a special gift—
grow up strong in what you are
remain strong in your background,
and your Ngarrungu identity
will never shift.

Dedicated to my second daughter Gabrielle Rahman, whose Indigenous name is Mowangka

Jabirr-Jabirr—original people of areas north of Broome, WA
Ngarrungu—Aboriginal/Indigenous Australian
Yawuru—original people of Broome

DEBRA ADELAIDE
Desiring the Unknown

There were three dreams, and two babies.

The first dream came when I was eight months pregnant. I stood beside a large glass window overlooking the sea. It was daytime. Light almost drowned me through the window. Standing in my loose garment, I took hold of my stomach. It lifted out lightly and easily, almost floating between my hands, as weightless as a balloon. I held it up to the window, high above my head, and the light entered the globe of my stomach, revealing its contents.

Inside the glowing sphere was a perfect baby boy. The colours were red, yellow and white. I gazed at this sphere for what seemed an age but was probably, in the way of dreams, mere seconds. Then I replaced my globe stomach and my baby back onto my hips and the dream ended.

When I woke I thought it very strange. Not because I lifted up my pregnant stomach to the light to see inside— that seemed quite normal—but because I knew I was going to have a girl.

In the second dream I travelled to the hospital alone, had my baby, and, still alone, returned to my car with the new baby bundled up beside me. I drove to my parents' house. Look, I said to my mother, I have a surprise for you, and to her delight I showed her my little parcel.

She peered at it. But she wanted to know, Was it a boy or a girl? That was a good question. I didn't know. So excited about bringing her the baby, I had forgotten to look.

So we laid the baby on her bed and unwrapped it. The folds of the blanket fell apart to reveal a tiny set of male genitals. Then I looked closer at my baby's face, which now seemed to resemble his father's features so much they were almost his in miniature. Again I thought it odd that I should dream about a boy when I was having a girl. Nothing else in these two strange dreams seemed as strange as this. In the last months of the pregnancy, everyone—including mere acquaintances such as Italian men in greengrocers', or the woman who sold me paint in the hardware shop—kept telling me I was having a girl. And I wanted a girl.

I don't remember the third dream.

My baby took a long time coming. The signs were there, but they were slow. It was 7.30 in the evening. I swallowed iron pills at the first obvious twinge because I thought I might need the extra energy. I had a hot bath. The twinges turned into contractions coming every half hour almost on the stroke of the clock. Every half hour for several hours. My husband and I knew we had to wait until they were ten minutes or so apart. I packed some food in my hospital bag and a few extra books. Then we kept a vigil to wait until it was time to leave for the hospital. We watched the television. There was a Sherlock Holmes film festival starring Basil Rathbone and Nigel Bruce. We watched every one until three am, my husband dozing on the floor and me wide awake, alert and confident. I had read all the right books and was going to have a pain-free birth.

Twenty-four hours after the first contractions I was buried in pain and such palpable emotional exhaustion it was like trying to breathe and move under the dead weight of the earth itself. This was nothing like the books had said. Nowhere had I read that contractions could be two minutes apart for hours and hours and hours.

The midwife sat crosslegged in a corner, knitting a huge shapeless garment. I don't remember her face, but I remember the size of the needles, and the raw sausage-pink colour of the wool.

Finally—when I was secretly hoping that someone, anyone, would walk into the birthing centre, take me away, anaesthetise me, cut this baby out and end this ordeal—finally the midwife raised her head at the subtle change in the timbre of my moans. She placed her knitting carefully on the table and said to me, Would you like to kneel here and have your baby?

Did this mean it was finally coming? Evidently so, for she helped haul me out of the beanbag which I'd been draped over for hours, panting like a fat desperate whale on a beach; she turned me around and I squatted on a mat.

I declined a mirror. It was enough to feel the incredible burning pain, the sign the body is stretching to hitherto unimaginable limits. I didn't want to witness it as well. But I willed my perineum to burst, rip, any tearing at all, as long as I could get this baby out. My sister sat opposite me and I saw in the shine of her beautiful eyes—the same eyes my baby was to have—the bright anticipation that I should have felt had I not been so consumed by exhaustion, so completely immersed in the dark vortex which ended where life, if it was that, began.

My husband had an art gallery. Mostly the visitors were artists, not buyers. One day his friend visited, with identical twin boys in either hand. They sat opposite him at the desk and stared unblinking with solemn black eyes, mechanically tapping with a pencil each, as if sending out coded messages. Giving birth, explained the artist friend, is just like doing one enormous shit. Then looking at the boys she added: In my case, two.

During childbirth some of the senses shut down while others become more acute. I saw very little beyond a point, but heard everything, even the late-night traffic out in the main street. I swear I still heard the clipped tones of Basil Rathbone as Sherlock Holmes. I heard the midwife say that my baby had a lot of black hair. And then I heard her say, That's the head out. I thought, That means the body will have to turn and it will be some time before the rest emerges.

But seconds later I heard my sister's quick intake of breath, a gasp of surprise, and at the same time felt the strangest sensation of all the sensations I'd experienced in the last twenty-four hours or more. A flood. A whoosh. Quickly, slickly, wetly, my baby's body followed the head in a final warm plop onto the mat in front of me, landing stomach side up.

Some years before, I'd read Germaine Greer's *Sex and Destiny*. She talks about the vastly differing experiences of childbirth, making the point that the process is never the same. Each birth experience is disorienting, unpredictable, again and again, for every birth, even for the same mother. She says that therefore wanting childbirth is a matter of *desiring the unknown*.

It was a boy.

I reached out and picked him up, calling him softly, crying with joy, My baby, my darling baby, I've waited a long time for you to come, oh my beautiful baby boy.

For I recognised him at once. I had been convinced I

was having a girl, but as soon as I saw my baby boy I thought, Yes it's you. This was the baby I had known for months and months, talked to, sung to, hugged tight, caressed and adored. The baby I had dreamed about after all. It was him, and no other. The *unknown*, but the baby I had *desired* all along.

So far it was his and my greatest achievement. Together we had written the complete works of Beethoven, scaled the Himalayas, flown to the moon and back, then around the earth several times for good measure. Nothing I had ever done was as clever, as beautiful, as pure or as perfect as this.

Now I knew how God felt, after the sixth day of creation. Why he had done it. I was a god. I was a goddess. I was God. I had commanded creation, said *Fiat Lux*, and witnessed life in all its glory. Had I also blasphemed?

Pulsing with emotions, I held my baby to my naked body and, like a miser with a chest of gold, frankly gloated over his miraculous perfection. We had prepared ourselves well with photo albums and textbooks supplied by the birth educator. We had seen illustrations of huge anonymous breasts swinging over vulvas stretched beyond imagination, culminating in purple gnomes held up in triumph, their knotty umbilici trailing like appliance cords. We'd seen the newborn in all their stark ugliness: crumpled angry old men faces, grey-blue blobs with bizarre misshapen heads, frog creatures of splayed hands and turned-in feet, dripping membrane and blood. We knew to expect a monster that would turn into something pliant and cuddly within hours after the vernix and mucus were wiped away, as the features relaxed, and as the soft plates of the cranium settled after the squeezebox ordeal down the birth canal.

But there was no vernix, no blood. He was not grey or blue or even oxblood red. He was pink, clean and perfectly formed, washed by the amniotic fluid which had gushed out minutes before he emerged. Shortly after I picked him up the placenta arrived. I gave birth again, and here was the monster, looking like something from the blood-splattered butcher's shop in Marrickville Road, which sells things like spleen and blood jelly. Yet the midwife handled it almost as lovingly as I my baby; she patted it, turned it over, pointed out the raw place where it had been attached to my uterus, invited us to admire its healthy colour and size. She pegged the umbilical cord then offered my husband the instrument. He cut the cord.

My husband's brother and father had died, so had a large part of my husband. We named our son for his dead uncle, his dead grandfather. So this first baby was a gift to my husband. My body conceived and grew, then gasped, screamed and sang, and at the end I was able to hold up my gift in sadness and in joy. Here, here he is, a little replacement for your love. It was and will remain the best moment of my life.

I know there were other people in the darkened room in those few holy minutes following the birth, but it was late at night and they soon left—my sister who, unknown to any but herself, was then carrying the embryo of her second baby; my friend who had dropped by after work thinking the baby was due any minute and had remained to offer a hand which I had unknowingly gripped vicelike for hours; the midwife who vanished into the dim interior of the birthing centre with her knitting needles.

All that remained were my husband and my baby and though we were that classic trinity, no amount of love, or acknowledgement of his essential role in the entire process, could make me agree that he felt as close to our baby as I. How could he? It was my body now dripping and throbbing with an ache that was to continue for weeks. My vagina torn and grazed. My perineum turned fiery red from stretching. My stomach, crumpled and crisscrossed with purple marks creeping out of the groin, and now flaccid like an old balloon which would never float again.

A long time ago—so long that I can't remember where— I read something by a man, recollecting his early childhood. He described his mother's breasts smelling like fresh-baked bread. I thought, What nonsense, how could breasts smell like new bread?

After my husband left us many hours later I snuggled up in bed to try and sleep for the few remaining hours before the hospital wake-up. I didn't sleep then, and I didn't sleep the next night either. On the following day, buzzing and hot-eyed from exhaustion, I went home to recover.

Partly it was the narrow hospital bed, the restriction of pillows, the noise. But mostly it was the sheer sensuous joy of having a new creature close beside me. I never knew until I had a baby just how many hours could be spent gazing in adoration. Possibly if I had been told, I would have dismissed it as sentimental mush, just like I had dismissed the now-forgotten author's description of new bread breasts. But now it became clear he was right.

All the birthing books and pregnancy guides in the world do not reveal this: a new baby smells as sweet and fresh as anything imaginable. A baby smells as wholesome and holy as creation. A baby's smell is far better than any favourite scent which you could name.

During those first weeks, I was enveloped in the aromas from my own and my baby's body. There are scent glands on the baby's head. Even if she were blindfolded in a room of babies, a mother would know her own baby from his or her smell alone. Months and months into our baby's life my husband and I would find ourselves leaning over his head and breathing in that warm baby scent.

All the baby books in the world do not explain your desire to do nothing but gaze at this new child, whether he or she is asleep or awake. They do not explain that you will spend hours draped over a cot stroking the head and breathing in, like an incense, that pure fragrance. Like the new bread simile, I had also once read that babies smell of milk and honey. A sickly image. But placing your nose close to those partly opened lips you smell the breath of your sleeping baby: it is achingly sweet and fresh, as if the child cannot be mere mortal flesh with its pungent odours, but made of something altogether heavenly.

The three wise men of the East brought gold, frankincense and myrrh as gifts to the newborn Christ child. He lay on a bed of hay in a manger in a stable. This is the earliest association I have of babies, of birth. As a child I listened to the story every Christmas, and every Christmas associated the time with certain smells: the stable I knew would have smelt of animals and manure, the hay like the drought-dry December grass mown in our long backyard. But what did the frankincense and myrrh smell of? Unspeakable mysterious oriental substances, so rare and precious they were only ever offered to this particular baby. Gold, that was in many stories. But frankincense and myrrh never appeared in any context except this, the birth in the stable.

And the second baby? This one squirmed and dug its heels and poked its elbows all through the pregnancy like the other, active though he was, had not. My stomach was much smaller this time, though I expected it would be bigger. Nor were there any dreams. This time everyone told me I was having a boy and I agreed. Once I had wanted a girl when wanting seemed to be of importance, but now having had one I knew that just to have the baby was enough. The pregnancy was different in other respects. For weeks at night somewhere during the second trimester I could not sleep: maybe that's why there were no dreams. Then in the final weeks when sleep had returned I would be woken by false labour—contractions painful but elusive, never forming a pattern, slyly vanishing when I got up to walk around the house, then returning just as I was dozing off again at two or three am.

Two days before the due date I was woken again, around midnight. This time I thought it might be the real thing, and while I thought I probably wouldn't have a twenty-seven hour labour again, was sure I'd be in for a long session. So I took aspirin and went back to bed. An hour later I was getting myself a hot water bottle and dismissing suggestions I ring the hospital. Yes, the contractions were certainly strong enough but I'd been tricked before hadn't I? I wasn't going to leave my warm house on a cold night just to sit in a hospital for another ten hours.

But I spoke to the midwife who listened to me breathing noisily down the telephone line through a couple of contractions. Then we bundled our sleepy son into his dressing gown, delivered him to the care of our neighbour, and set off for the birthing centre, which at that hour was mere minutes away.

This time there was no fatigue, and there were no tears, drugs or moans. This time I was in charge of my body and I was delivering my own baby. I felt the power I had wanted to feel the time before, but had been too exhausted. The pain ripped through my body in great convulsive waves just as before, but now I felt carried along on the superhuman strength of those waves, not overcome by them. My body was a great and complex machine, I was the driver, and we were travelling fast towards a brilliant and beautiful destination. I walked around the birthing room, paused to catch my strength leaning against the bed or a chair, then walked around again, a perambulating pod ready to burst.

Half an hour after we checked in I was on my knees on the floor feeling for the lumpy head of my baby. The midwife pierced the membranes for me, and a tiny amount of amniotic fluid seeped out: nothing like the flood from my other birth. She stopped me when the head emerged, to unwind the umbilical cord from my baby's neck where it was coiled twice like a noose. Then we took it slowly, and slowly my baby emerged, after several minutes of gentle persuasive pushes.

They say the vernix is white but of course it is grey. My baby's back was turned to me. It was alive, because it was moving, but otherwise it could have been a half-formed clay sculpture abandoned by its creator. Several strings of blood and slimy mucus clung to the infant here and there like a web.

It had been a minute or two: a long period in the suspended-time world of the birthing room. Gently I turned the little body over and saw through the sticky garment of its womb-coverings that my baby was a girl.

I always knew it was a girl, whispered my husband. I'd had no idea, but was so glad because we'd had great trouble deciding upon a boy's name for a second time. And of course, secretly, I was desperately hoping for a girl.

This baby smelt profoundly earthy, as if she had indeed come from a claypit and not my womb. She smelt of rusty blood and the waxy vernix. She felt warm, damp and firm as a tomato. I wondered what it would be like to lick her clean, like other mothers in the animal world. I settled for placing kisses over her, rubbing my face close to hers. I don't know if my husband ever felt this elemental physical closeness, to either of his babies. One day I will ask him.

The midwife took the baby off and wiped her with a warm cotton blanket, removing most of the coating and much of the earth-blood smell. Quickly and deftly, like midwives do, she wrapped her as she was in another blanket, and when I held her again I saw that her hair, free of most of the vernix and blood, was curly light brown. Later when I washed her I left a smear of blood behind an ear, to remind me.

This time I had done it absolutely right. I was the textbook Kitzinger mother, the resourceful strong one always in control. The mother I'd despised the first time round, seeing her prance around the hospital afterwards in jaunty tracksuits while I slunk and groped my way from bed to bathroom, nursing a throbbing groin, a chronic exhaustion, a sense of guilt and even failure.

It's a bit like a book, said friends who'd done both and should have known better. Like *what*? No books I produced ever took this amount of pain. And on the positive side, I was also convinced that they didn't involve this sort of genius either. Anyone could go off and write a book. Not just anyone could give birth. At least, not to my two splendid babies.

The first baby resembled the women in my family, and was named for the men in my husband's.

This second baby had the fair, rosy colouring of my husband's father's family, and we named her with my mother's middle name. We also gave her the name of my own grandmother, whom I could never have known, for she died when my father was four; hers was a floral name, suggestive of fading fragrance, and darkness, and Keats's quiet *easeful Death*.

My baby daughter is past the age of three. That tender place on the back of her neck, which looks so vulnerable but is really a strong stem—the same place on her brother which I also held to my lips and nostrils again and again, like an addict unable to get enough of the drug—is now covered by curls the colour of cornsilk. I scoop the hair up, to expose that place. I do this from pure selfish indulgence. I touch it with my fingertips, press my lips against the sweet skin. I fondle her, I breathe her in.

We still gather them into our arms and take them into our bed, just so we can satisfy our senses.

This is it. This is the real thing.

As for heaven, if it has a smell, I'm sure it's better than the legendary frankincense and myrrh, and very similar to the smell of the back of a baby's neck.

The third dream I have never remembered. I wonder if it's because I am living it, or if because, like most dreams, it didn't matter.

Women who want the experience of childbirth are in the curious position of desiring the unknown.
Germaine Greer, *Sex and Destiny, the Politics of Human Fertility* (London: 1984)

MONICA TRAPAGA
Gardening and Giving Birth

I t is said that mothers forget the pain of childbirth so that they will continue to procreate. I've never felt that is altogether true. I don't think that the pain a mother feels in those moments of labour or those nine very uncomfortable pregnant months leading to delivery can ever be forgotten. I do feel, however, that the joy a newborn brings far outweighs those feelings of pain, so the temptation to bring another child into the world is great.

I've had two children. They are ten years apart. They have different fathers and were both incredibly different birthing experiences. My first child, Lily, is now ten years old. I had Lily when I was nineteen, unmarried (though I had a partner) and full of dreams to become an actor and singer. I was living in the country, on a property my parents had purchased. It was a magnificent piece of land with no electricity, no hot water, but plenty of fresh air. We grew our own vegies, cooked on a wonderful wood stove, and basically lived in a very peaceful environment.

I'd had a healthy pregnancy apart from the initial three months, during which I spent my every waking hour projectile vomiting. I'd lost three stone (19 kg) and by the time I'd hit my second trimester I weighed seven stone (44 kg). I kept thinking, How could I possibly be keeping a baby alive when I was throwing up every ounce of nutrition that I swallowed?

Apart from those first three uncomfortable months everything ran smoothly. We went to baby classes, both the conservative and the not-so-conservative ones. The hospital classes demonstrated the importance of nappy folding, which we diligently practised on plastic babies. The other classes gave very insightful information about the whole ordeal of delivery. We read everything from Michel Odent and Sheila Kitzinger to Ina May Gaskin's *Spiritual Midwifery*. I felt very ready to have my first baby although I wasn't too anxious. I quite liked being pregnant, so when my waters broke two weeks before my estimated time of delivery, I was surprisingly calm.

I had been gardening in the vegie patch. I cruised into the house, sat on the loo and asked my partner, Ian, for a scotch. It was my first drink in nine months and certainly did the trick. We calmly rang the hospital and spoke to my doctor who told us to come in immediately. But we had been waiting for our electrician to come that afternoon to connect our power and I had no intention of going anywhere until the small matter of electricity had been taken care of. Naturally my doctor was not pleased with this decision. My waters had broken at 4.30 pm and by six o'clock there was still no sign of the electrician—so we decided to go to the hospital. While driving there I remember saying to Ian, 'Who knows, this might be a false alarm'. Little did I know what the next two hours would bring.

We arrived at the hospital and filled out all the relevant forms. I had an examination and was asked whether my contractions had begun. I'd been having pretty strong Braxton-Hicks for two weeks and I hadn't noticed anything different, so I said no. At about six o'clock I had my first serious contraction. We told the nurse who said, 'Get ready for the long haul'. I sent Ian home to have a shower and call the family. It was at that moment—as Ian walked out the door—that the contractions started with the force of a charging bull. I was alone and had no intention of engaging the company of the other mothers in labour. I remember climbing into the shower and crouching, letting the water beat down on me as the contractions got heavier. After about an hour of this I told the nurse that I was beginning to bear down and that I was ready to push.

The nurse was a rather large elderly woman who took

great pleasure in telling me that it wasn't possible and that I was going to be here for many more hours. I remembered then what they had taught us in the alternative baby classes: if you feel the urge to push and you're not fully dilated, to slow everything down, get on all fours like a dog, rock back and forward and pant. The only place that was carpeted, however, was the TV room where all the expectant fathers had gathered together to smoke cigars and watch the footy. Naturally they were a little concerned with my behaviour—I must have looked like a rabid dog. Ian returned and was a little shocked to hear me say, 'I'm ready to deliver, now go tell that cow if she wants me to have it here in front of all these men I will! Otherwise take me to the delivery room'. I was then given an examination in the middle of a contraction and was relieved to hear the bovine-like nurse proclaim, 'Oh my God, you're fully dilated! I'll call the doctor'.

We made our way to the delivery room. I hopped up on the bed, lay in a reclining position and pushed with all my might. Our doctor arrived about ten minutes before I actually delivered. He channelled my energies and helped me focus on the right parts of my baby, and although that sounds strange it was a tremendous help. The force of that baby was incredible and, with a few pushes, Lily arrived, gorgeous and pink. The time was 8.35 pm. I immediately put her on my bosom and she suckled away while I delivered the placenta. I was overwhelmed with maternal instincts and even though she had come with such force, I can't recall feeling any pain except for the needle containing local anaesthetic that was administered, enabling the doctor to stitch a small tear.

When I found out I was pregnant again ten years later I thought it was going to be a breeze after such a painless first delivery. With hindsight, I now know what a difference ten years can make to your body.

When I fell pregnant this time I hardly suffered any morning sickness and began to put on weight immediately. The second time around I was very happily married to Julian. I was busy working with a singing and acting career. We were living in a large renovator's delight with electricity and hot water, but not much else. My work-load was manic, to put it mildly, and Julian was working full-time as well. I worked right up till I was eight months pregnant and by then I'd had enough. I had been pregnant through a very hot summer and had swollen up like a sausage about to burst. The day I went into labour I was 72 kg (that's about twelve stone). I was incredibly anxious, tremendously uncomfortable and very impatient. I was so big I couldn't sleep. The day before the baby was due we all ate a huge meal at our favourite café and wandered up and down King Street. I finally decided to swallow some castor oil with orange juice to bring this baby on. We'd tried everything else. Everyone had given us the same advice: have sex, try nipple stimulation. I think people forget that having sex with a nine-month pregnant woman is like doing circus tricks with a two-humped camel.

By that Sunday, I was well and truly desperate. We decided to do something positive and plant out the backyard. We bought a stone birdbath and planted lavender and poppies all around it. Julian dug while Lily and I planted until we were ready to collapse with exhaustion. In the late afternoon I had a hot shower, ordered some take-away and later sat down to watch 'Sixty Minutes'. This time I felt definite contractions. Lily, Julian and my brother Ignatius all tried to time the contractions although no one could remember whether to time from the beginning or from the end, or whether to time the length of the contractions or the time in between! Julian went to have a shower while I looked for the only pair of shoes that still fitted my swollen feet, only to discover our dog Elvis had turned them into beef jerky. Lily ran around and grabbed the various things we needed. We called the birth centre and a man with a thick Middle Eastern accent answered and told me the midwife was having a baby. I didn't care, and wasn't about to hang around to see whether this was true or not. My waters broke while I was hopping into the car. My husband scaled the fence and tore his jeans wide open to reveal his jewels. I was in my socks, having never recovered the beef jerky shoes. Everything was a lot more hurried and a lot more intense.

When we arrived at the birth centre the poor midwife, who was supposedly having the baby, greeted us looking totally stressed—she was awaiting the arrival of two more midwives as she had two mothers delivering at the same time. I was number three. We told her that we were fine and could look after ourselves. Julian went to administration while I filled up the bath and climbed in. I was there for about an hour while the contractions were approximately two minutes apart. I got out of the bath for a while so I could have an internal examination. The midwife told me that I was only four centimetres dilated. I was terribly disappointed as I thought that I was much closer to delivery than that. I remember the contractions then started to intensify. They were stronger and more frequent. I hung on to Julian, bent my knees and rocked back and forth. I felt a lot more pain this time. Julian kept a heat pack on my lower back and constantly reassured me as I huffed and puffed. I was determined to be in control this time. Having always remembered the stitching as the only painful part of my first delivery, I didn't want to be stitched again. This time when the urge to push came, I tried instead to pant through it. I must admit it was the most painful experience of my life. It felt almost as if this baby didn't want to come out; as if he was happy being shielded in a protective environment, away from our frantic life.

I was back in the bath as the water was the only soothing thing. At one stage my midwife said, 'He's a little stuck ... at the next contraction I'll see if I can move the cervix back.' I remember howling and letting out very primeval screams. Finally came the push that revealed his head ... boy oh boy, I would have gladly been cut in two if it meant delivering the baby sooner. There is a strange sensation with a water birth as the baby's head remains underwater while you deliver the shoulders. The three and a half minutes between delivering his head and those footballer's shoulders felt like an hour. This was a much bigger baby than Lily. Then the greatest relief of my life, that super contraction and out he popped into the water.

I pulled him up and held him to my chest, crying 'Hello darling'. My husband always says that this is the moment he'll never forget. It was like two lovers seeing each other after a long separation. In a way, that's how you feel. You've carried this person around for months, and half the anxiety comes from the frustration of not being able to hold your loved one.

Well, Atticus was a hefty 3.9 kilos. A healthy, hairy, devilish little boy. Both births had been so totally different. The similarities, however, are the beautiful memories that come with a newborn. That delicious smell they exude, that's almost like vanilla shortbread. That dreamy sleepiness that only comes for those first few weeks. That velvet skin that is as smooth as satin and as fragrant as freshly baked bread.

That totally dependent feeling you have when they are in your arms—it is like no other feeling in the world.

DOROTHY JOHNSTON
A Christmas Story

Sophie has her eye on a house. She walks past it every day, and she talks to Melissa about it with the mixture of make-believe and confession that forms the major part of her conversations with her baby daughter.

It's the nicest house Sophie has ever seen. Sometimes there is washing on the line at the back. Once she heard music coming from the front room, but she's never seen the people who live there. She has no reason to suppose the house will be sold, but this doesn't stop her from saving for a deposit. 'Just you and me,' she says to Melissa. 'Think of it!'

Melissa tries to roll over in her stroller, which is adjusted to the lying down position. She arches her long neck and smiles.

'Just you and me,' Sophie says again, this time her voice scarcely a whisper.

Great trees shade the house. One stormy afternoon they watch them, crossed and contorted by the wind. And the house stands up. It just has to.

Melissa's stroller has a hood, though the strong rain slashes underneath it. Sophie turns her own face to the sky, and the rain falls splat on it. 'Look!' She shouts in triumph. Melissa begins to cry.

Sophie wonders whether the house has any sort of special history. Simply being old in a new suburb maybe gives it this. It doesn't have the design of a farmhouse, and she can't imagine it ever having been surrounded by sheep. It is constructed of rectangular blocks of stone, the colour of the French mustard in the deli section of the supermarket. Sophie decides that constructed is the right word. She imagines the blocks being manoeuvred into place, the sweaty muscles of the builders.

There are other large houses on the hill, houses whose paintwork is barely dry, whose new brickishness is not yet softened by trees. Sophie barely glances at them while she pushes Melissa's stroller energetically back down the hill.

The flats where Sophie and Melissa live have no gardens. A strip of cement and gravel separates them from the street. If there was a neon sign out the front there'd be nothing to distinguish them from a motel. When the sun's good and high, it seems as if the walls and roof of each flat are shouting to it, 'Come on down here! Burn me up!'

Sophie puts Melissa down for her nap and remembers the morning she was born.

'I've seen her Soph! Soph! I think she's hungry!' exclaimed Melissa's father Darren, his face half hidden behind two great bunches of carnations.

Sophie's stitches hurt. She winced and said, 'They're lovely. You went into the nursery?'

'Through the glass!' cried Darren. 'I'll tell the nurse!'

Sophie smiles as she recalls Darren returning behind a nurse pushing a hospital crib. He hammed it up, pretending to waddle like the nurse, and Sophie held her breath because Darren did unexpected, gross things when he was feeling out of place and nervous.

Sophie was glad when the nurse handed her Melissa and quickly left, throwing over her shoulder, 'Not too long or you'll wear her out.'

'She thinks I'm *way* too young,' Sophie said to Darren, who went red in the face and asked, 'It came straight away like that, the milk?'

'Oh no, not for three days. There's something else, I forget its name. You can hold her in a minute.'

Darren rubbed his hands together. Sophie could see how they were sweating. He took the tightly wrapped lozenge of hospital blanket from her and bent over their daughter's tiny raw face, covered with wrinkles like an old book cover. 'Sweetheart,' he whispered. 'Darling.'

Sophie sighs and wonders what Darren's doing, where he is right now, in what part of the country.

Melissa's hair is powder fine. Through it Sophie can see her daughter's milky skull, each stud and wrinkle, the fontanelle still wide, a slip for fingers. When Melissa wakes in the night, or when Sophie wakes, imagining she hears her daughter, with her nightgown soaked and her breasts aching, she thinks of the house on the hill and the big old trees surrounding it. Knowing the house is there lessens the chore of getting up in the night. When Melissa wakes hungry and Sophie feeds her, whispering to her, she thinks of the trees singing hush-hush and takes their voices for a lullaby.

She spends whole days playing with Melissa, days that begin at five or six in the morning and go on unbroken, with the same slow rhythm, until nine or ten at night. 'My darling,' she whispers, bending and kissing Melissa's toes one after the other. 'My best love.' Melissa grins and turns her feet in Sophie's hands.

There are no divisions of time apart from the ones Sophie decides to make. She doesn't like watches or clocks. She lets the kitchen clock run down and turns its face to the wall. She sleeps during the day. She and Melissa can be asleep or awake at any time: they are on a twenty-four hour shift. It's like swimming underwater, Sophie thinks. You don't see or hear or feel things as clearly as you do above the surface. You hear with a perpetual hum in your ears, but the things you see are different, and some are beautiful.

The memory, or rather the *idea* of Darren appears to Sophie very strange then, and she has to struggle to recall the outlines of his face. She discovers that loving Melissa isn't a substitute, but a thing existing entirely in and for itself. Do all mothers feel this? she wonders. She wonders what she's going to do for money, and confesses to Melissa that it doesn't look as though Darren's coming back.

The woman in the corner flat is Sophie's friend. Her name is Mrs P. She has wide Polish cheekbones and a settled smile. Mrs P is a widow whose son used to live in Canberra, she tells Sophie, and he always took her out in the car—the Fyshwick markets and all kinds of places. Sophie doesn't know whether this was a long time ago, or recently. Mrs P is vague on this point. She loves Melissa, and talks to her in a mixture of languages which Sophie calls Ponglish.

Sophie, Melissa and Mrs P catch the bus to Fyshwick to do their shopping, and Sophie leaves Melissa in the act of reaching both arms up to a round, ripe rockmelon. She says to Mrs P, 'There's a shop I want to take a peek at. Too far to push the stroller. Meet you at the pet shop over there? I'll hurry. Thanks.'

Alone, she approaches Capital Delights like a prowler might, a street-walker of a different kind, a splinter of nervousness running up her spine.

A computer place, a Sleep Doctor, and a Pink Panther printers occupy the same cul-de-sac as the massage parlour. Small bushes encircle the computer place, spiky Fyshwick bushes backing out of white pebbles, with bits of black plastic showing through. It's like the area around the flats—lots of concrete—but cleaner, and the buildings are huddled together.

Sophie takes a deep breath and rings the bell.

'New girls are always welcome,' says the woman who opens the door and invites Sophie in. She has a cigarette voice with a deep crack in it somewhere.

'The best range of services in Canberra,' she boasts, showing Sophie around, then arranging herself on a tall bar stool behind a white-topped desk.

Sophie can work Friday and Saturday nights if she wants to, but Sophie says maybe just Friday for starters. She doesn't want the woman, who says her name is Mrs Dawson, to know she has a baby daughter.

Thankfully Mrs Dawson doesn't ask her any questions. She tells Sophie not to worry. An older girl will show her the ropes, and she'll be fine.

Mrs Dawson has long curly red hair, and is wearing a low-cut blouse which shows the wrinkles round her breasts. She says that businessmen travelling interstate feel at home here, and asks, 'What'll I call you love?'

'Sophie. I prefer that to Sophia, which is my real name.'

Mrs Dawson finds this funny for some reason. She

throws back her head so that Sophie can see the make-up on her neck, and laughs.

For an instant Sophie hates Mrs Dawson. She feels small and stupid. But Mrs Dawson goes out of her way to be pleasant. Sophie can wear what she likes to work. She doesn't have to wear lace nighties or suspender belts or any daggy stuff. She can stick to her own name. That's fine too. The only thing is—'Get yourself a G-string, love. Because some clients only want a G-string massage.'

Everything at Capital Delights is overdone, Sophie decides, hurrying back to the pet shop—from the name to Mrs Dawson's make-up to the fuzzy red-textured wall-paper and the fountain up the front. And the bedrooms, which are something else.

During the week, she buys a green silk G-string from a lingerie shop, and on Friday night she shows it to Mrs Dawson, hoping she won't notice that her hands are shaking. Mrs Dawson pronounces it 'very stylish'.

No one has touched her since Darren left when Melissa was seventeen days old. No one except Melissa. Her breasts have been Melissa's, her mouth, her hair, her hands—all have been her baby's.

Sophie particularly doesn't want any of the clients to comment on her stretch marks, which are fading.

There are no buses from Fyshwick to Tuggeranong at five o'clock on a Saturday morning, so Mrs Dawson calls Sophie a taxi. The driver changes lanes without needing to, coasting effortlessly across two sets of broken white lines which gleam dully under arc lights. The sun is a green glow over the markets, strengthening second by second. Sophie wonders when they turn the lights off. She's never been out on the road at this hour of the morning.

On one side the grass has been cut, but on the other it's taller than she is, waving in the dawn wind, each single stem weighted with its head of ripe seeds.

The driver doesn't try to make conversation. He tells her it's been quiet for a Friday, and that's it till he flicks off the meter and says what she owes him.

She's still amazed when she opens her bag to see the roll of notes; it's like she's already forgotten. She's glad she's sitting in the back seat, and tells him he can keep the change. He flashes surprise, but she's gone, out and away, running across the concrete.

She grabs Melissa and kisses her, *kisses her*. Melissa squirms in Sophie's arms, while Mrs P yawns and says she's been no trouble, but next time don't come charging in and wake us up eh? Sophie laughs and says she won't.

'Iss only few steps from my door. I vill brink her ven she vakes.'

A few hours later, when she goes to the shop, Sophie's sure *it's written all over her*. But Mr Loukakis says, 'G'day, Soph, how's the nipper? What'll it be?' He doesn't even say she's looking tired.

There are two girls at the Capital who've been with Mrs Dawson for years and years. They're called the twins, and they laugh in identical cigarette voices. They do doubles and are incredibly popular.

The twins become Sophie's friends. They show her how to bring a client off quickly, and teach her little tricks of concentration, to fake an orgasm sometimes but not every time. They laugh at private jokes, and treat one another with a courtesy that Sophie thinks of as old-fashioned, until she realises she's never met anyone, old or young, like them.

'Tits are worth something,' Mrs Dawson says, 'but a good personality's worth more.'

Sophie's breasts are swollen with milk. She wonders how she could ever have thought that Mrs Dawson wouldn't notice.

At home, she cups her breasts in the palms of her hands and lifts them. She turns side on to the mirror. Pears, she thinks. Pears, personality. Personality, pears. Then she thinks his name, just that one word. *Darren.*

'So fuck you,' she says aloud.

One afternoon Sophie has a cup of tea and a slice of carrot cake at the School of Arts café, where the tea costs thirty cents more than at the take-away across the road. The café is tastefully decorated for Christmas, and there are reserved cards on all the larger tables. Sophie sits at a small one in a corner. What the hell, she thinks, staring back at two middle-aged women at the table next to hers. I can *afford* it. She lifts Melissa out of her stroller and feeds her a few crumbs of carrot cake. The women look on disapprovingly, while Melissa gags and Sophie rushes her outside.

Sophie's glad Melissa isn't old enough to ask questions. She pays Mrs P well for her night's babysitting, and Mrs P never asks questions about Sophie's Friday night job, not even half-framed Ponglish ones, for which Sophie would have to find half-deceitful answers. She feels the need to ask each week, 'Okay for Friday?' and Mrs P nods in businesslike agreement.

Early on Saturday mornings she pushes her door shut behind her, telling herself there's still time for a couple of hours' sleep before Melissa wakes up, but, tired though she is, she can rarely go to sleep.

She has to wait till Monday before she can take her money to the bank. Until then it sits in a drawer in the bedroom. She has opened an account in another name at a bank in Kingston. She hates keeping the money in the drawer all weekend. She hates opening the drawer and seeing it. It makes her feel dizzy, like she's standing on some high place, on a ledge, and the ground starts to shake. But she loves the thought of it sitting in the bank. She has a new relationship with the house she's saving for. She doesn't visit it so often, but at night it fills her dreams.

Total fire ban days follow one another monotonously through December. The city is surrounded by elephant-high yellow grass just waiting for the right spark. The loose guttering on the flats buckles and burns. The thin walls hum at the end of each day, and their inhabitants pant like dogs.

On Friday nights, Sophie walks into the Capital's incredible, freshly watered luxury. The fountain in the reception area is like the rain that always passes too high overhead, the rainclouds that won't be tempted earthward.

Johns with grey skin order champagne, 'Because it's Christmas'. 'Cheers!' they say to Sophie, and smile and raise their glasses. Sophie tries to empty her breasts of milk before each client, but even reasonable men begin to dream of drinking from them, and she is no longer shocked.

Outside the parlour, her head aches from the dryness—from air that snaps back at you when you breathe, and sucks the last moisture out of the ground with a hiss and a crackle that might be laughter.

One Friday night, Sophie is standing at a bedroom door saying goodbye to a client. He's wanting a last kiss and Sophie's smiling her 'it's-over-for-tonight' smile when she catches, around his shoulder, a glimpse of light brown hair, and athletic hips under stone-washed jeans.

She pulls her head back, biting the inside of her lip so hard she cuts it.

'You've hurt yourself—what is it?' The client plays for time.

'Nothing,' Sophie hisses, stepping back.

But she knows it's no good. Before ten minutes has passed, she's opening an adjacent bedroom door and Darren is saying, 'Well well, turned the hooker have we Soph?'

He closes the door behind them, and takes his time to look her up and down. 'Well, well, a little bird told me, but not till I saw it with my own eyes ...' He turns as if speaking to an invisible companion. 'Sophie's standing here like the cleaning lady. Will it help if I sit on the bed?'

Sophie clenches her fists by her side, feeling his eyes all over her like suction caps.

'I thought I might have a nice cool drink,' Darren says.

'They don't serve alcohol.'

'An upmarket joint like this? Don't kid me. I'll have a Jack Daniels with lots of ice.'

'No.'

'Yes,' he says. 'Otherwise I might have to make a fuss.'

Sophie comes back with Darren's whiskey. She watches him taste and nod approval. The wall lights give him a halo. Brown hair curls away from his temples, and above his head, and it's like each curl owns its special bubble of light.

'What've you done with Melissa?' Darren asks.

Mimicking his voice, Sophie says, 'How *is* Melissa? I

miss my daughter and I love her and I have a responsibility and from now on I'm going to stay around and be a father to her.'

Darren laughs and has another drink. 'Sit down Soph,' he says, patting the bed beside him.

Sophie watches Darren's throat; she plays that trick she plays when she's with a client, of fixing her eyes on some harmless part of him, and keeping them there. It doesn't work.

'Talk!' she insists. 'Where've you *been*? How dare you run out on me like that? There's such a thing as *child support.*'

Darren laughs again, with his head thrown back, and despite herself she's laughing too, laughing with him.

She sits on the bed. 'Seriously Darren.'

'I'm here aren't I?' he replies. 'And besides, it's Christmas.'

Mrs Dawson lifts her eyebrows, and stares at Darren and Sophie through rings of black eye make-up; and though part of Sophie is already out the door, wings on her heels, another part is held by the older woman's eyes. Though she cannot exactly read their expression, she knows Mrs Dawson is not surprised. For a second she wonders what Darren has told her.

Then Mrs Dawson says, 'Aren't you going to introduce me?'

Sophie flutters her hands and cannot speak. When

Darren follows Sophie out the front door, Mrs Dawson winks at him and says, 'G'night beautiful. Come again.'

When Sophie puts Melissa down on the bed beside her father, Melissa waves her legs and grins.

All the next day, Saturday, Sophie watches them together—the way Darren walks to the fridge for juice for Melissa's bottle, the muscles under his skin smooth as olive oil. He's like a jaguar or a cheetah, Sophie thinks. Darren sits on the end of the bed and smokes, and shakes his hair so that light flies out of it. When Melissa spits out her juice, Darren laughs and says, '*I* know what you want.'

The anger towards *her*, the *mother*, is gone, his young man's rage that she has done this thing, and done it to *him*. Strange, Sophie has never doubted that Darren loved his daughter. Or has she? Her mind is playing tricks.

Darren settles Melissa into her cot for her afternoon sleep, talking quietly to her, while Sophie stares into the cracked bathroom mirror.

Then she lies on the bed next to Darren and stares at the wall, at a dirty patch of plaster, and wishes it was dark. She thinks that if it was only night right now, she could read Darren's mind.

He closes his eyes. She doesn't know if he's asleep, or pretending to be. She whispers, 'When Missy wakes up, we'll show you the house.'

They stand under one of the big trees on top of the hill, in deep shade, not trespassing or anything, just on the footpath. They stare over the fence. As usual, the doors are shut, and there's no one there. But Darren likes the house.

Melissa gurgles whenever Darren's hand, or any other bit of him comes within her field of vision. She kicks out with her bare feet and lifts her arms to him.

Walking back to the flats, Sophie wonders if perhaps it's money that is making Darren restless. She knows it's a mistake, but she says, 'Well, what would *you* have done?'

Darren doesn't answer. Instead he says, 'Hey Soph, want an ice-cream?'

She hesitates, then answers, 'Sure.'

She humps the stroller up the milk bar's single step, calling 'Hi!' to Mr Loukakis, who's serving a gaggle of kids.

'What would Melissa like?' Darren asks, smiling indulgently down on his daughter's head. 'Since this is a special occasion!'

'Idiot,' says Sophie. 'She can't eat ice-cream yet.'

Mr Loukakis laughs. Darren does too, then he asks for two Drumsticks. Mr Loukakis hands them across, and takes the money, as if they're the most important customers he's had all day.

Darren doesn't want to go back to the flat. 'How 'bout a beer? The Terminus. Soph! Come on, they've got air-conditioning!'

Darren lifts Melissa out of her stroller and nurses her while Sophie goes to the ladies, wets her hair in front, and straightens it. She notices that there's nowhere to change or feed a baby.

They stay till ten, when she's aching with hunger, and Melissa's fallen asleep in her father's arms. After a few horrible moments of indecision, Sophie has taken her outside to feed her. Darren's drunk, but he can still walk and talk normally, which amazes Sophie all over again because she's practically forgotten his abilities in this department.

Sophie changes Melissa and puts her in her cot. When she comes back, Darren is dead asleep, diagonally across the bed.

Light brown hair falls across one amber cheek. Sophie bends and kisses it. Darren's real, sleeping presence lets out all the memories of before Melissa was born, as if the bad times have scarcely happened.

Sophie strokes a finger along Darren's arm, that creamy olive place. She's always loved his skin. She kisses his elbow. She is glad he is drunk and feels nothing. She wishes he would never wake up. She thinks, What if he hangs around long enough for Missy to fall in love with him: what then?

JULIE CLARKE
Happy Birthday

There are two extremes in the current approach to birth: 1. Birth is a sacrament, an enacting of a wider truth, an ennobling experience from which you gain a level of autonomy that women as a group have lost. When a woman fully experiences birth, she learns much about herself; and, 2. Wake me when the hairdresser arrives. In between these extremes lies the norm: 'Doctor, I'd really like to have a natural birth.' To which comes the response, 'Of course, dear. You can have the baby hanging from a chandelier if that's what you want.'

About thirty per cent of women who have this conversation with their doctor end up with either a forceps or a caesarean birth. Not one of them has her baby hanging from a chandelier.

For something so normal, an everyday occurrence intrinsic to their sex, women remain mind-bogglingly ignorant about the process of birth. Many of us believe the only way a baby can safely get out of its mother's body is with the help of a rich male who wears a bow tie, puts us in stirrups and orchestrates a shiny array of electronic gadgets and sophisticated chemical cocktails, not to mention the good old scalpel. But some experts are claiming that 'the birth machine' is out of control and that technology is used inappropriately and excessively before, during and after birth. Other experts are claiming that, in a different social climate, nearly all women could safely, and much more happily, be having their babies at home with a midwife.

Twelve years ago, I chose home birth, infuriated by the patronising and rigid approach of the hospital into which I was booked. Since then, concern about the way hospital births are conducted has been growing and central to this concern are medical problems caused by medical intervention. Births at home are important because they fly a flag that reminds us that, wherever we have our babies, we don't necessarily have to depend on machines that go beep.

Wendy Savage started her medical life as a conventional obstetrician in the UK and had her own babies by the book. After long experience with women in labour and watching many outcomes, she changed her technique from 'hands on' to 'hands off' whenever possible. She has observed that many women get anxious just going into hospital. The screams and shouts of other women, the hospital smells, the association with illness and death can all cause a rise in adrenalin that can interfere with, and even stop, the natural course of labour. Without wishing to convert people who feel safer in hospital, she cites evidence that suggests birth proceeds differently in familiar surroundings.

Savage is a hero among London mothers, and a legend in her own labour ward. She has presided over thousands of births in the London public hospital system, and tends to wear boiler suits instead of bow ties. Like many other experts, she no longer looks at birth as a medical event, but as a sexual one, deeply affected by emotions and the physical surroundings. 'You would not say to a young couple about to consummate [their love] for the first time, "Now get in there and do it on that high narrow bed under these bright lights with all these strangers watching, and you've got three hours, otherwise we experts will step in and do it right for you".' Nor should you in birth, a culmination of sexual life.

Elizabeth Davis, a Californian midwife and author, has observed the emotional states that occur during labour and their effect on the hormones which regulate and 'drive' it: 'Birth is a passionate, sexual experience. In fact, of all the events in a woman's sexual life, birth can be the pinnacle. It's not a tidy little physical event where you can keep control.'

The prime hormonal agent in labour is oxytocin. It is the hormone that's released with breast stimulation, breastfeeding and orgasm, which is why it's called the 'love hormone'. It also makes the uterus contract. But the release of oxytocin can be blocked by a rise in adrenalin, something which happens to many women when they are admitted to hospital. This is why it is common for labour to slow or stop after a woman arrives at hospital, even though she has been experiencing strong, regular contractions beforehand.

Sheila Kitzinger, the Oxford anthropologist and birth educator, also reminds us that while we may be postfeminist yuppies on one level, we are still mammals when it comes to giving birth. 'Creating a nest that meets the needs of the mother and her newborn is something that all mammals do, unless, like animals in a zoo, they are in captivity. Women in our post-industrial society are effectively captive in childbirth.'

The revered Kitzinger is one of the leading proponents of a return to home birth. Her sane, humane and relaxed approach to birth, the massive international sales of her books on pregnancy, birth and baby-raising, coupled with the great respect in which she is held, make it hard for doctors to dismiss her as a loony extremist, despite her fierce attacks on the management of births in hospitals (one article is entitled 'Birth as Rape') and her graphic language: 'I have no doubt at all that some men become obstetricians because they want to get their fist up a woman's vagina. They want to control women and birth.'

During one of her talks for nurses, doctors and midwives at a home birth conference held in Sydney in 1992, one young male medical officer from a Queensland hospital described how the obstetricians at his hospital talked jokingly among themselves of their work as 'slash work' and 'gash work'. And when Kitzinger asked if anyone in the room had witnessed, during labour in hospitals, treatment of women which they felt to be inhumane or cruel, about 300 hands were raised.

Here is a common hospital scenario:

Anna Jones (not her real name), twenty-nine, has just gone into labour with her first child. She is one of those women who has said to her doctor, 'I'd really like to have a natural birth.'

Niggling pains, becoming sharper and sharper and coming at regular intervals, are contracting her uterus. She has been waiting for this day with happiness and fear. She believes she is fully prepared. At birth class, Anna and her husband, John, rehearsed what they would do. There's a full tank of petrol in the car to get them to the hospital, a purseful of change for the public phone so John can phone friends and relatives with the happy news. Anna's bag is packed, with nighties and the tiny clothes the baby will wear when they bring it home. Anna has become very attached to her doctor during the monthly ante-natal visits. He has been very kind and reassuring and has even said she can have a beanbag during labour. The ante-natal classes she has attended have given her a basic understanding of the mechanics of birth and she has learned different positions helpful for labouring, as well as what hospital procedures she can expect.

At the reception desk she spends fifteen minutes filling out the admission forms, then a midwife comes down to escort her up to the labour ward. She is taken first to the prep room where a midwife examines her, feeling her tummy to check the strength of the contractions and the position of the baby, and performing a vaginal examination to check on the dilation of the cervix. Then two belts strapped around her abdomen are hooked up to the electronic foetal monitor to check on the baby's heartbeat, and the midwife leaves the room to phone the doctor. Anna and her husband are left alone for thirty minutes. She feels scared. Her adrenalin level rises, and this knocks out the oxytocin, the hormone which drives the uterine contractions, and they stop.

The midwife returns and checks her progress. 'Oh dear, you seem to have slowed down, Mrs Jones,' she says. 'I'll take you into your own room now, the delivery room, and you can settle in.'

The private delivery room is painted a pale pink and has floral curtains. But its centrepiece, a high stainless steel bed, is what catches Anna's eye. As does the stainless steel trolley, the oxygen unit on the wall, a resuscitation unit and, reminding her of the reason she is here, a plastic cot. This room is where Anna is to labour and deliver her baby, but despite the cheery curtains and cheery midwife, she feels fear tightening her chest. 'I'll put a beanbag on the bed for you,' says the midwife kindly.

As a child, going to hospital to have her tonsils out was a terrifying experience for Anna. She feels just as powerless now.

Then her doctor arrives, and she feels a bit better. 'So, what's happened to these contractions?' he asks jokingly. 'Don't worry, we'll give you a drip to get them going.'

A Syntocinon drip, a synthetic form of oxytocin, is set up and attached to Anna's arm. It makes the contractions come on very strongly, and although she had hoped for a 'natural birth' and had liked the sound of a 'drug-free birth', she really needs pain relief, and the midwife gives her an injection of pethidine. This makes her drowsy, and although she is still feeling pain, it feels much further away, as does reality. Thanks to the drip, she is now having very strong contractions every five minutes. The dose is increased every twenty minutes until the contractions are coming about every two minutes. Time passes in a blur for Anna. John holds her hand, watches the print-out from the foetal monitor machine, and wishes there was more he could do. Four hours later, the doctor returns and decides to break the waters. This is a way of speeding things up and of checking on the baby. But he does not tell Anna what he is doing, as he thinks it might upset her. So, during the vaginal examination, he nicks the thin membrane that surrounds the baby in its amniotic sac. There is a small amount of meconium in the waters, which means the baby has pooed in the amniotic fluid, and could be distressed.

To monitor the baby, a scalp electrode joined to a wire is clipped to the skin of the baby's head. The wire comes out of the vagina and is attached to Anna's leg and then to the electronic foetal monitor. A wide belt is wrapped around Anna's stomach to record the contractions. Her movement now is very restricted and she is frightened and disoriented. Her husband encourages her to have the epidural anaesthetic that the midwife has suggested. She has to curl up on her side and not move while the anaesthetic is injected into the base of her spine.

Anna is now trussed up like a turkey. There are two drips, one to keep the contractions going, the other one to keep her blood pressure stable. There is the wire going out of her vagina attached to the baby's scalp, plus the belt. But at least, now that the epidural is taking effect she can't feel anything. She is numb from the waist down. Her husband is on a chair by the bed, reading the paper, relieved she has calmed down. Every twenty minutes or so, a midwife pops in and says, 'How are you going, Mrs Jones?' and looks at the monitor. But Anna is going to be here for another eight hours before anything major happens.

Home birth proponents say that educated, enquiring,

articulate women, just as often as those who've had less opportunity to acquire the confidence to question authority, are befuddled by obstetric mystique. And in planning how they will give birth, seldom think of it as anything other than a risky medical procedure.

Midwife Elizabeth Davis has become a voice for approaching childbirth as a 'personal growth experience', which is what it always was in the old days, as well as, frequently, a personal death experience for many mothers and babies. The history of childbirth has always been a history of risk and suffering. It is only recently that public health has improved to the point where birth can be considered generally a safe procedure and its metaphysical aspects savoured. 'Birth is a pinnacle in a woman's life and you can't go back and do it over again,' says Davis. It was through her own experience—from a hospital birth in the 'dark ages' to having her second child at home—that Davis decided to train to become a midwife.

'The difference between the two births was an amazing learning experience. In the first, I was ordered around and told what to do ... The second time, at home, my midwives enabled me to discover my own way to get through birth. You reach a point halfway through a labour when you discover birth is bigger than you are, and that the only way out is through, and the key to that is surrender. It can be transformative and ecstatic.'

I don't know about the ecstatic part, but transformative, certainly. It's a rite of passage, in which a woman is transformed from a well-groomed, well-organised, self-centred, carefree, child-free person into the exhausted, poo-wiping, milk-sodden, love-ravaged hero that is a new mother.

Says Davis: 'A woman who finds a way to get through birth learns a lesson that is hard to come by in our civilised society ... that women's way is power with, not power over. Birth fully enables a woman to experience and know firsthand a lot of power. The first six weeks with a baby is the hardest thing you'll ever do; a positive birth experience sure helps this along. If a woman can ride it out and go with it, she's got the best possible start to being a fierce and determined mother.'

Anna is still trussed up, immobile, and awaiting a visit from an expert who will decide what is next to be done to her. Philippa, another woman whose labour pains got going at the same time, has decided to have her baby at home. She thinks she'll react much better in her own surroundings than in hospital; her pregnancy has been straightforward, and she has read enough to convince herself that a normal birth is not an illness that requires hospitalisation. But she has booked into a hospital, and can get there in ten minutes if it becomes necessary.

Everything is ready at Philippa's, too, and when she feels her contractions starting and is convinced they are real, she phones her sister and a friend who come over and polish and vacuum, fill the house with flowers and put on a pot of chicken soup. She phones her husband, Peter, who leaves work to drive home, and her midwife, who tells her to keep a record of the timing of the contractions. 'Keep walking!' is the midwife's advice, so, with her friend, she walks down to the park, plays on the swings, and thinks how good it will be to bring her baby there. But the contractions are getting pretty strong, taking her breath away. They walk back to the house, stopping to lean on something when each contraction begins; her husband pulls up with a screech of brakes, looking excited and nervous and making awful jokes about Swiss army knives and boiling water. Hearing via the next excited phone call that the contractions are now regular and strong, the midwife decides it is time to come.

Philippa, who has been looking forward to this birthday party, is now starting to find the whole thing more than a joke. Every four minutes her abdomen is racked by a pain that is like nothing she has ever experienced. She could think of it as unbearable, and lose control, but she has prepared herself and starts testing out ways of dealing with the pain, letting out short panting breaths, concentrating on a tapestry on the wall. Then the pain stops, and she feels normal, can walk around, and even for a minute, forget the whole thing. And then, 'Here comes another one!' She leans over an armchair, while her husband massages her back. She counts the threads in the tapestry on the wall, and reminds herself that each contraction is opening her cervix further, letting the baby out.

Arriving at the front door, the midwife hears a sound that bodes well, the low, controlled moaning of a woman in serious labour. She quickly checks Philippa's dilation by feeling the cervix; she is four centimetres dilated. She listens in to the baby's heartbeat which is strong and regular. Philippa thinks the whole thing must surely be nearly over—pain can only get so intense, after all—and hearing that she still has six centimetres to go is briefly depressed. 'Think of it as work you have to do,' says the midwife. 'It's the hardest work you'll ever do and the most worthwhile. And you can do it. Every contraction brings the baby closer. And we're right here with you.'

Philippa takes a deep breath and takes control of herself. Her surroundings are calm and reassuring. Night is now falling, the room is warm and dim, Peter has lit the fire, there is the scent of daphne, an atmosphere of time standing still, although Philippa certainly isn't. She is being heroic, still walking between contractions, joking and trying out odd positions like hanging over the back of a chair, crouching on all fours, but wondering how much longer she will be able to cope, because now when the pain comes it is impossible to believe that a human body would do such a thing to itself.

But another part of Philippa's brain seems to be taking over, disassociating her mind from her body just enough for her to be able to keep going, as the relentless and intensifying pains visit and revisit her body. Wearing only a T-shirt, bathed in sweat, with Peter giving her sips of fruit juice, getting in and out of a hot bath, occasionally retching, Philippa endures. Peter holds her, strokes her, holds her gaze when it seems she is going to lose it.

She feels that she is off in some other reality, from which she may never return. There is nothing but the pain coming and going. On the other hand, she is not frightened, she feels relaxed and secure. In between quick checks of her dilation and the foetal heart rate, the midwife is back in another room, reading. 'I'm sick of this,' Philippa realises. 'I've had enough. And get that stupid look off your face,' she snaps at Peter. 'And everyone can go home. I can't take it any more. I'm not having any damn baby.'

The outburst of anger is a classic sign of transition, the end of the first stage, which means that her cervix is fully opened up. Soon it will be time for her to push the baby out. The midwife will be able to attend to any tears that require stitches. If necessary, she will administer an injection that makes the uterus contract so the placenta can be expelled.

In the hospital, eight hours later, Anna is still lying there, unable to move, with various strings coming out of her vagina and running down her leg or up her arm. She is feeling a detached sense of unreality; her husband, reading an old magazine, is feeling not only tired and drained, but irrelevant. The nurse is keeping a close eye on the foetal monitor.

Finally, Anna's cervix is fully dilated. The epidural is wearing off. She can feel the pressure of the contractions, but no pain. 'Okay Anna, push now . . .' says the midwife. But it's hard to push when she is flat on her back and can feel nothing. Push what? Push where? With her knees up to her ears, held up by her husband and the midwife, she tries, but she is exhausted and disoriented and, after an hour, there is still no descent of the baby.

The obstetrician decides to do a forceps delivery. Anna's epidural is topped up and she is catheterised so that her bladder is not traumatised by the forceps. Then her legs are strapped up into the stirrups (which had been folded away under the bed). She is covered in green drapes to create a sterile field, and the doctor puts on wellington boots and a green robe and mask. A stainless steel bowl is placed beneath Anna's vagina and the doctor inserts forceps the size of salad servers into her vagina before taking surgical scissors and enlarging the size of the vagina with a cut so he can pull the baby out with the forceps.

Not long afterwards, Anna's husband is away at the public phone, calling friends and relatives with the happy news. Anna is in bed, holding her tightly wrapped little bundle with his pointy head and bruised face. She is shaking uncontrollably and tears are running down her face. A nurse brings her a cup of tea.

Anna Jones has just had a fairly standard hospital birth.

Sheila Kitzinger is 'devastated by the misogyny and lack of compassion shown to women in labour in hospitals'. She suggests that much postnatal depression is a normal reaction to an experience which is, for many women, a violation and a mutilation. 'In some hospital births, as in rape, a woman is stripped and tethered, her sexual organs are on display, and attention centred on the space between her legs. So many woman say afterwards of their doctor, "He never looked at the top half of me." Attendants are crowded round with all the attention on the vulva, as though at an airport carousel waiting for the baggage to appear. And after such an experience, complaining about a bad hospital birth can be just as damaging as reporting a rape.'

It is interesting to look at a male doctor's view of the same type of birth as Anna's, to remind us that they are not monsters, but rather boys with toys. Wrote Dr Steven Ford, a UK general practitioner, in 1987: 'On the occasion of our own daughter's delivery we enjoyed the whole panoply of high-tech obstetrics, and very effective and reassuring it was, too—an epidural that allowed my wife to sleep fairly soundly until the start of the second stage, a rampart of comforting, unblinkingly vigilant monitors that emitted a gentle variety of hums and clicks, a drip to fend off ketosis and dehydration and maintain the labour's momentum. A superlative demonstration of technology in an appropriate, supportive, caring, safe-guarding role. The actual delivery was accomplished with forceps, and the episiotomy was repaired while we embraced the child and each other.'

Such techno births as this would never be allowed to happen anywhere near the French birth guru, Michel Odent, the doctor at whose birth centre in Pithiviers women labour in the privacy of warm, dark rooms with access to warm pools for pain relief and relaxation. 'It's a male attitude to try to control nature, it's male to try to dominate life, including the process of birth, and it's a male attitude to be fascinated by technology,' claims Odent, adding waspishly, 'many husbands in the hospital births concentrate most of their attention on the beeps and buzzes of the electronic foetal monitors.'

Odent insists we must now enter the 'post-electronic age' for birth. 'We have to adapt home birth for a modern, urbanised society and learn how to combine what the privacy of the home can offer with the facilities of the hospital when they are necessary. And what we need more than anything for this new age of birth are midwives.'

Home birth midwives tend to be rugged individualists, not surprising since they are treated like political dissidents and, in the past, were not uncommonly burnt as witches. They are passionate about their work, their faces shine with an inner light, probably because they get to see a lot of calm newborn babies, who do actually come trailing clouds of glory. Ask anyone who has been at a good birth.

The baby comes, the gateway between the material and spiritual world has opened, and something changes in the room, even in the whole house. For hours there is undeniable glory around.

Ina May Gaskin, perhaps the world's most famous alternative midwife, would agree. 'Yes, of course. And I and many other midwives have noticed birds and animals gathering around at natural births. Often, at a farm, when a baby's coming, I look up and see that a couple of cows have stuck their heads in at the open window.

'It's just plain sense, really, helping babies get born. You create a good feeling of warmth and relaxation. Laughter helps the sphincter open. The most common problem at birth is what they call "failure to progress". So I ask the woman if something is bothering her, talk it through. Failure to progress is nearly always some psychological problem. Or I get her smooching with her man, get them to try a bit of nipple stimulation, might even suggest they make love if the waters haven't broken. A bit of kissing and cuddling can get the oxytocin pumping. If a woman in birth doesn't look wildly beautiful, someone isn't treating her properly. I treat a labouring woman as a goddess.'

A midwife at a home birth is taking on a huge emotional and medical responsibility. She may have to sit around twiddling her thumbs for twenty-four hours or more before the birth. And in the event of something going wrong at the birth, she bears full responsibility. If the baby dies at hospital, it can be said, 'We've done everything possible';

Julie Clarke

if it dies at home, it is said, 'It would have been saved if at hospital.'

Sue Sagewood, a midwife practising in the Blue Mountains area west of Sydney, says, 'You've got to have a lot of drive to be a midwife, and to choose home birth. We've all been disempowered by the medicalisation of birth. Feminists have chosen not to pick up the birth issue. They've run with body image, with work, but not birth, because motherhood has been seen as a subjugation, and children seen as a millstone around a woman's neck.'

Being a midwife has its lighter moments, though, Sagewood reveals. Like the times when, while practising in the inner city, the noise of labour upset the neighbours. 'One hot summer day, I was out in the garden with a client who was well into labour. She was on all fours, rocking back and forwards, and moaning very loudly. Then the dog started howling. The people next door called the police.' Another time, a gay couple who lived in the flat above a woman giving birth, and whom the new parents had never met, knocked at the door next day with gifts. It emerged that they'd heard every stage of the labour and had found it one of the most moving experiences of their lives.

That reminds me. I left Philippa a few pages back getting rather jack of the whole drug-free birth business, and ready to start pushing her baby out. Lucky for Philippa, her endorphins have come to the party. Lucky for her,

268

too, that she has gravity on her side, as she squats, with her husband behind her, supporting her under the arms. The midwife is down on the floor, watching the baby's head crowning. 'Come on, you're nearly there. One more push.'

Philippa screams as she experiences for a few moments the utterly agonising, impossible stretching of her perineum as the head makes it out, and the never-to-be forgotten feeling of a tiny body slithering, through her, into the world.

Soon, she is sitting up, cradling her baby, looking into her eyes. This is as joyful as the human condition can get. Physically, she feels as though she has run a marathon, but is already forgetting what she has been through. She says to Peter, 'This is the way it was meant to be.' The room is glowing in the firelight. Love is in the air. The placenta is delivered. The cord cut. Everyone sits by the fire and drinks champagne. Then Philippa, Peter and their new baby fall asleep together in the family bed.

A Melbourne doctor, Peter Lucas, who, like Philippa, sees birth as a sacrament, persists in keeping births at home as part of his suburban family practice. 'Like the frog being slowly boiled, oblivious until he dies, this community is dying spiritually. As a community, we have been alienated from ourselves, our feelings, and our biology. In the service of the machine and profit. If women reclaim their bodies, our children, once imprinted, will follow. The way we give birth is an opportunity to rehumanise, to change the world.'

This is radical stuff. And I believe it. But, still, I feel nervous. I talk to my doctor, a woman in charge of many of the births at our local country hospital, where intervention rates have dropped in the past ten years to some of the lowest in the country, partly due to the influence of this doctor, along with that of the home birth movement in the area.

'It's true that a lot of doctors become obstetricians because they couldn't get into surgery, or because they hate women and it's true that a lot of doctors still believe they're God. But a lot of women still want to believe that doctors are God ... Many women actively want an obstetrically managed birth. It's what they expect.'

Anna, walking slowly down the corridor, is passed by a young woman who is obviously soon to give birth. They smile at each other.

'Good luck!' says Anna.

'Thanks,' says the other woman. 'How was it for you?'

'It was okay. You'll be okay.'

'I hope so,' says the pregnant woman. 'I'd really like to have a natural birth.'

Further reading:

Elizabeth Davis, *Heart and Hands: a midwife's guide to pregnancy and birth*, Berkeley, California, Celestial Arts, 1987 (2nd edition).

Ina May Gaskin, *Spiritual Midwifery*, Summertown, Tennessee, Book Publishing Co, 1990 (revised edition).

Sheila Kitzinger, *Homebirth and other alternatives to hospital*, Sydney, Doubleday, 1991.

Michel Odent, *Birth Reborn* (trans. Jane Pincus & Juliette Levin), London, Souvenir, 1984; *Entering the World: the de-medicalization of childbirth* (trans. Christine Hauch), New York, M. Boyars, 1984.

Wendy Savage, *Savage Enquiry, Who Controls Childbirth?*, London, Virago, 1986.

ANNA MARIA DELL'OSO
Harvest Day

One night years ago I fretted that my period was overdue several days. From my bed, through the open curtains, I saw the full moon grinning down at me. In the moonlight I began to cramp and suddenly I understood my woman's rhythms for the first time. *The Moon, my Mother.* Since then I have always looked to the moon to check on the inner timing of things down there. Our moon-shaped clocks are merely the little fish from that great yellow sea.

The moon was new on the evening of the day the medical centre doctor told me I was six weeks pregnant. I saw the thin milk ring above the trees of the park near our house as I jogged through the wet summer grass. Round and round, ten laps or five kilometres: for a few nights I took my body through its paces as usual. I felt sick and confused but I didn't know yet how to yield to this force so I clung to the routines of the taut life that I had made. It was strange to think of my tiny foetus child afloat on a huge amniotic sea, too new even to know it had begun upon that old and ruthless journey. Like some random second of a ticking clock, it was a measure of almost nothing and yet it moved fiercely towards the hour of its being.

By the ninth month, I was huge. I was a big fruit. I was squelching heavy, drooping, sleepless, immobile. I had put on seventeen kilos and I was just there waiting. On the deepest level I knew nothing of what was to happen. I just seemed to spill out circular, a boundless belly. In my mind however I knew everything, or so I thought. In the manner of the day, I had read all the books and attended two sets of classes, dedicatedly practising to confront the unknowable.

At 11.10 on a Sunday night, I was reading Sheila Kitzinger's *Giving Birth, How It Really Feels*, when my waters broke.

Dream-knitted night, web-black thick
the phone spasms
that other cord, the moon
huge, full, heavy
unfurled, a calendar, a command
her great roundness slipping
huge fruit
down, down

Nothing had prepared me for the great gushes of blood that accompanied each virtually imperceptible contraction. None of the books mentioned anything like it and I hadn't heard of it from any of the countless women I had talked to. I was frightened, especially for the baby: not a good start. As it turned out, it was nothing much at all. A tiny corner of the placenta had lifted off; there was no immediate danger to me or the baby. However at the time no one was taking any chances: the labour ward sister said to come in at once.

The hospital was around the corner, in the street across the local park; I had planned to walk my way through it in the first stage of labour. I decided to give the bleeding ten minutes to abate; I was keen to stay home and go into the labour ward towards morning because I wasn't really yet in labour and I wanted to sleep while I could. I was already tired and I knew I wouldn't rest in hospital because I can't bear fluorescent lights. My husband and I walked out into the soft night, taking our dog who was highly skittish and nervous of the new smell of me. Fruit bats flapped through the trees. We made it once around the Moreton Bay figs when I realised it was not a good idea to hang about: I was flowing like a tap, not clear or pinkish waters but bright red.

Apart from anything else, I couldn't think what to do with myself at home because we had already used just about every towel and sheet we had.

The labour ward sister had said over the phone that,

as we lived so close, we might arrange to go home again if everything was all right. Once in hospital however, I was gripped in the system's rules and procedures, not to mention the huge stomach-belt contraption that measures contractions. The baby's heartbeat was strong, my blood pressure was normal, the contractions were very weak, barely pre-labour strength. The medical staff were evasive about the bleeding, which made me anxious as I was neither a child nor a fool but a woman who had spent nine long months carrying this fruit: later I learned that evasiveness is routine hospital behaviour if they can't get an official statement from your specialist; that is, they'd rather worry you to death than tell you honestly and promptly what the hell, if anything, is going on.

The only way I deduced that things were a little unusual but basically okay was because I was still feeling well and fit despite the blood gushes, and the staff dispatched me to a prenatal ward for the night and left me alone till seven am. By then I had been in labour for two hours, since five am . . . but I hadn't slept a wink all night.

Obstetrics had calculated my time as three days before the full moon, a reasonable guess, I thought. I was so certain I would be delivered at the full moon that I had made appointments right until the last minute. No one believed me except my obstetrician, a wise woman with two children of her own.

I was delivered of my child at an hour or so before the

daytime rise of the full October harvest moon. I felt pleased that it was the one thing that had turned out according to my hunches rather than my studied expectations, the one thing that was purely instinctual and not out of a book or calculated.

What I hadn't dreamed of was that it would take thirty-two hours (excluding a few hours of the mild warm-up stuff) to see this child born. In labour the babe had turned from the classic head-down-forwards into an odd position: ironically my pelvis was large enough for it to muck about in this way. I was working hard but not getting very far: the midwives were sorry to tell me how little I was dilating. A night, a day, another night and a morning went past as I was squeezed and thrown by that big fist of pain. I saw myself as I truly was, a piece of flesh pummelled by the life force, just a speck of life in the universe, unimportant other than as the carrier of the ceaseless chaos. I hung on the breath, *a-pant-a-pant-a-pant*, scream, *a-pant-a-pant-a-pant*, scream ... That is all there is, everything else is illusion. Among the screaming and the heaving, the clutching for the gas, the pleas for the anaesthetist—*get him, get him now, go and get him, get him, get him* NOW— I caught the edges of my helpers' eyes and faces and wondered, *Don't they know this?* We live on a precipice— a knife's edge!

In the end, after two nights and another sunrise, after the walks, the different positions, the monitors, the drips, the showers, the gas, the epidurals that worked, the epidurals that didn't work, the offers of pethidine fiercely rejected—NO FUCKING PETHIDINE—(there is always the one thing you will not have no matter what. I suddenly understood why torture is useless. There will always be the thing never to be relinquished. The thing that can't be budged dwells in an Orwellian Room 102 of our psyche, next to the object in Room 101 which we cannot bear and will do anything to avoid. I couldn't believe I was prepared to conk out rather than have the one thing I couldn't accept. I was amazed how my brain said no, no and the ultimate NO, and my body just had to obey.)—

—In the end all I had was my own breath. On the bottom line I found just this: in and out, light and dark, yes and no, one and two, this and that, you and me, birth and death, inspire, expire. In my ears it sounded as though all the world was reduced to the in and out of breath, light and fast blows on top of the battering waves. Tiny snatches—*a-pant-a-pant-a-pant-a-pant*—from the great Breath: In and Out. My husband leaned down to breathe with me, my sister-in-law breathed on the other side but it was my friend Veronique, who had given birth to a boy four months before me, to whom I clung. She seemed to know exactly what to do and say and was relentless, riding over the top of my abuse and despair, accepting everything but giving me her breath to breathe, never stopping, *a-pant-a-pant-a-pant-a-pant*, In and Out.

On the monitor the baby's heart beats, beats, beats.

> *O darling it's your harvest day,*
> *love's harvest day*
> *the threshers sweat, the scythes are coming*
> *a-pant-a-pant-a-pant-a-pant*
> *a-pant-a-pant-a-pant-a-pant*
> *O darling, the scythes are coming . . .*
> *my God, oh God, oh God, my God*
> *a-pant-a-pant-a-pant-a-pant*
> *Oh God, my God, oh God, my God*
> *o-when o-when o-when o-when*
> *a-pant-a-pant-a-pant-a-pant*
> *a-beat a-beat a-beat a-beat . . .*
> *O-babe, o-babe, o-babe, o-babe*
> *let me see you, let me see you*
> *let me see your face, let me see it*
> *O darling, o, o, o, o darling,*
> *o darling come to us, come to us, come to us*
> *O darling, it's your harvest day*
> *love's harvest day*
> *the threshers sweat, the scythes are coming . . .*

We're making acceptable progress, that's why I'm not sectioned thank God; somehow we are moving along but it's slow and I'm exhausted from the even slower labour of the previous day. I'm in a bad way but I'm so proud. I'm so proud of that kid because his/her heartbeat has never wavered, not once. Or so I think. During the night while I doze with the first epidural, the baby's heart dips. My husband is asleep; my sister-in-law notices and calls the midwives. An oxygen mask is strapped to my face and I breathe, confused and unknowing. David later told me that I was told why but I can't believe it. I don't remember the heartbeat dipping. How could I forget something like that?

I roll over. The baby's heart beats, beats, beats.

I sleep for four hours. I sleep for a lifetime. I sleep the sleep of a hundred years. It's like drowning, my life dances before me in a kind of storybook sunset: little coloured bits of times and feelings jingling like a kid's rattle in the light behind my closed eyes.

The summer before we decided to make the second big decision of our life together and start 'a family', I had a dream.

I am in a long queue outside the Exhibition Buildings in a dream Melbourne that is nothing like the real place. There are all kinds of people jostling outside, waiting to take a series of examinations. I wait in the milling crowd, rocking a pusher with a baby inside. People turn to stare. A woman bends down and smiles. 'My God,' she says, 'but she's so pretty.'

I stare down at the baby. It is the first time I have noticed that I have a baby. I look closely at her. Pretty? Yes, I think to myself with some surprise: yes, she really is quite beautiful.

The woman asks, 'And what's her name?'
I smile. It's obvious.
'Rebecca.'

Early in the morning the epidural wears off, leaving me
in the middle of brutal contractions. I am in a raging
storm. With renewed vigour I concentrate. I am full of
hope but after only an hour and a half, I am as exhausted
as I ever was. I am told I have developed a slight fever
and seeing that by now I am hooked to surely almost
every contraption modern medicine has made available
to the labouring woman, I decide to go the whole hog
and demand more epidural top-ups. What the hell ...
stuff natural childbirth ... I've done my best and a bit
more. Fifteen hours without pain relief—and without the
best painkiller of all, the knowledge that you are getting
close to giving birth—is enough for anybody surely. Surely?

Yet I'm feeling confused, ashamed and betrayed by my
body. A sense of failure together with a touch of female
bio-posturing rages through me: women have babies all
the time—what's the matter with YOU? At the same
time, I know I'm being unreasonable: it's not my fault, or
anybody's fault, that the baby has turned into a posterior
transverse position with her head flexed. At the same
time I'm thinking, why me? At the same time I know the
answer is why not me—and be grateful it's not a lot
worse. At the same time I feel that having a baby has
been the biggest mistake of my life: stop the labour, I

want to go home and try it again in a few months' time—
or maybe never! At the same time I'm fearful for the
child and I don't care what the medical staff do to ensure
both of us come out of this alive and well. At the same
time I am enjoying the relief of this epidural more than
anything I've ever experienced and I almost—yes, I'm
going to say it—I don't care what it might do to me or
the baby in twenty minutes or twenty days or twenty
years so long as I can get away from the pain NOW.

The baby's heart beats, beats, beats. The big fist of pain
throws me from one end of myself to the other.

*Contraction by contraction, the invisible cord pulls us tighter:
Moon, mother, daughter, baby. Thirty-two years apart,
contraction by contraction, I am still linked to my mother. We
are again sharing the childbirth bed as I am rocked in the same
cradle of pain that saw me into the world: I have inherited the
pattern of this labour from her, Fate has handed us the baton
of this long, long race and now it is my turn to run with it.*

*My birth was my first original story from her, my first
knowledge of women's business and my first gothic horror tale;
unlike all the other stories, it was not set in once-upon-a-time
but a definite date in 1956 and had no ending: it grew along
with me like a heartbeat to follow me into death. Every time
I exasperated her—which was quite often as I was a 'difficult'
child—the story would unfold, tailing off with the oldest of
mother's curses: 'may you have a daughter like you.'*

To my astonishment, the epidural top-up does not 'take': I am left stranded on my back, unable to move from the waist down, as the contractions break over a corner of my pelvis. This is worse than no pain relief at all. I can't move, I am trapped like an insect under a gigantic pin. The anaesthetist is at an emergency caesarean, he will be back in twenty minutes. In my world all that means is another fifteen contractions. It may as well be never.

If I could walk I would throw myself out the window.

A-pant-a-pant-a-pant-a-pant, a-beat-a-beat-a-beat-a-beat, o-when-o-when-o-when-o-when . . .

She is twenty-five years old, she speaks no English and she has been labouring alone in a bed at Queen Victoria Hospital for a day and a night. Her husband, the only other kin she has in this foreign country, is not allowed to be with her, even if it were the custom among her people, which it definitely is not. Even so, he would be willing to be there because he knows her aloneness, the lack of women at her side. Instead he waits on the other side of town sick with fear, not daring to miss a day at the factory.

Doctors and midwives walk in and out of her vision, murmuring to themselves. She is a New Australian, she doesn't understand anything they say. So they say very little. Flat on her back, she is trapped like an insect under a gigantic pin. Is she dying, is the baby dying, why is it taking so long, what will happen, what are they doing? In elaborate sign language, a midwife tells her that her baby will be born in a few hours. Hours. It may as well be never. If she could walk she would throw herself out the window.

She doesn't know how long she has been screaming. A midwife comes in with a needle. 'When you wake up,' she says, 'you'll have your baby in your arms.'

With the help of forceps I come into the world greeted by the midwives and doctor whose name is on my birth certificate. My anaesthetised mother is unable to be present. My father was not allowed to be present.

In visiting hours that night my father presses a slip of paper to the nursery window to be shown his firstborn. He sees a red-blue bruised bundle like a squashed plum. He is so shocked the nurses have to reassure him there is nothing the matter with me and that I'll look prettier in a few days . . .

If I were a student over again, I'd study to become an anaesthetist. It must be gratifying and good for the soul to be able to ease pain for a living. How wonderful to see a labouring woman's eyes light up with love at your footfall. How blessed to be the most beloved person in the room. Not the husband, not the helpers, not the midwives nor even the obstetrician gets the affection, the gratitude, the passionate look of welcoming joy as does the anaesthetist.

Yet modern chemistry is not giving me a free ride. There is no relief until the epidural is re-sited. By then, even the anaesthetist is reluctant to give me yet another top-up. I insist.

In the long gullet of this labour, I have come to digest a contempt for the puny world of men. Even for the strongest of them, the marathon is only two hours, weightlifting but a few seconds of exertion. The average woman in her first labour will go six times the two hours of the marathon to give birth. There is no turning back, no dropping out of the race, not even the option of simply collapsing: once a woman steps into the great gullet, once she is squeezed in there by the big fist, something must be spat out, an outcome which is never any less than life or death. A woman labours until her child is born: the power, wherever it is coming from, is relentless— greater than life, greater than death. For a woman like me, a father's daughter, a daddy's girl who has spent a long time in the world of men, this comes as more of a shock than it should be. My understanding of work, of the verb to labour, *comes from the way men measure it: heaving weights, climbing Mount Everest, fighting wars, commanding companies or running a country.*

Now I know the ordinary woman in labour does much, much more than that. All those things of the world that I valued and feared, that I complained of, that I made such a big deal about, are nothing compared to what I am facing in labour. Nothing. For hundreds of years of our history, men have been able to con women into thinking that they're weak, that they're oppressed and have to be liberated because

*women's work is nothing, any fool can do it. What a hoax.
All that baiting about why there are no women artists or
composers, no women generals or women on the boards of
companies, when the question should have been why there are
no great women rapists, mass murderers, cut-throats and
warmongerers, no great male nurses, homemakers, child
rearers. Oh what a load of bollocks and conniving it's all been.
Now there are a generation of women who've done all that
alleged tough men's business and will continue to do it all:
we've flown the planes, we've been on the boards, we've made
money on the stock exchange, we've been in the parliaments
and now we know: bearing and raising children is harder.*

Seven centimetres. The entrance to the world is almost
open. Only a finger's breadth remains between the cave
and the light. Such a little distance to be born, such
an immense journey for mother and child. Despite the
overwhelming physical, animal work of the labour, I can
now feel a stillness above the waves. This child is
coming from a long way away, not only from deep within
my body but some other place: Mystery, Night, Soul;
whatever it is, I know it is real. It is being called, I
know it is.

Seven centimetres. I have to hang on but I am afraid
because I know I can't be safely given another epidural
top-up. Now I know what it is to face the end of the
tether and have to stretch it some more. Later, much
later, I will be glad I have known this. Now that I know

my power I feel I understand all women and I know all pain.

I used to have a lot of ideas about things I had never experienced and I suppose, for someone who is naturally inclined towards ideas and the life of the mind, I always will. Now I will at least try to distinguish between thinking about life and living it, between opinions and feelings. Ideas, opinions, theories, philosophies, beliefs are just that: ideas, interesting, illuminating things that can and must change like chameleons in contact with instinct, feeling, experience. Otherwise how can there ever be any compassion?

I used to have a lot of ideas about the bearing of pain, for instance. During this labour I experience it. Of course, I am bearing it for a purpose, a joyful greeting: there are two of us and I am at the ripe harvest moon of my life. Yet in the midst of my labour I have a sharp sense of what it must be like at the other end of the continuum, to be dying alone under the withering moon in this pain.

Those people who oppose euthanasia should put their bodies where their convictions are. I have a fantasy that the objectors enter a chamber where they are required to endure the simulated pain of those who can't bear it any longer. The moralists who come out of that chamber with their rigid cruel beliefs intact might possibly have a right to them. All the others who capitulate will surely be glad of the opportunity to know finally that great chasm between morality and wisdom, between law and compassion.

During contractions a midwife walks in clucking her tongue. 'Poor dear, you're doing it the hard way.'

I snatch a breath.

'Oh yeah?' I scream out, 'SO WHAT'S THE EASY WAY?'

The midwife is taken aback. Then a smile slowly spreads across her face.

'The next one.'

My obstetrician is sitting at the foot of my bed. The time has come: either I am fully dilated and she delivers by forceps or she does a caesarean. She says she can't stand to see me like this any longer. Put this way, I don't feel too badly. I sense her valuing of what I have tried to do. I am not just a contracting uterus with a badly positioned baby. I can see she knows the meaning of this for a labouring woman, the weight of it. I am so glad she is there.

The examination is swift but it's a long moment as I lie trying to prepare myself for the idea of surgery, the idea that I have laboured all these hours only to undergo an operation I could have had at the beginning (supposing that we had the benefit of hindsight which we didn't). All this effort wasted: what a cruel blow. I try to swing my mind back to everything I have read about coping with caesareans, I try to be humble to this force and just accept what it decrees. I try to think of how safe and easy it will be for the baby, to be lifted out like a peach from a syrupy tin ... All the while my still rebellious body and soul squirm *please, please, please ... just let me finish the job ...*

The last thing I need now is for someone to say, Why don't you just get knocked out and get it over and done with? I know because it's the sort of thing I might have said before I experienced this labour and understood. Do you tell a swimmer in the middle of her stroke: why bother? Do you tell an artist as she paints: why are you doing this? Do you tell someone drowning: hey you look ratshit, do you want a Valium? In the middle of this storm I don't want to hear any God-how-awfuls, should-have-dones, might-have-beens, don't-worries, forget-about-its, think-positives, next-week-you'll-be-partyings and other bullshit ... I don't want to be distracted and offered platitudes, I want one hundred per cent concentration on what is happening NOW ... I am at the wall, by the chasm, at the crossroads, in the deep wave's crest: I am where I know control is an illusion, right up against the heartbeat of chaos and that this is NORMAL, this is what our lives truly are, only in the daylight world most of us can't face it and the rest of us are too arrogant or too blind to believe it. Birth and death are normal, suffering is normal, uncertainty is normal, joy and despair are indistinguishable and normal, gold coins are paid to the ferryman on both sides of the river—paid from what you value, not what you can afford—and that is absolutely normal ... Each contraction now brings me to see with incredulity: how is it I have lived thirty-two years and not known any of this?

I have a chorus by my bed of husband, sister-in-law and woman friend, all singing 'yes, yes, yes' to my moans. Around me I have a litany of my labour: miraculously what could have been a trauma, a dark thing, just random pain squirming poor and cruel into the void, is lifted into the oldest of all songs of creation.

Being with someone, murmuring along with their heartbeat, breathing with them is a lost art. The true midwives of birth and death, those who keep vigil at the bedposts, are rare. They are people whose eyes are accustomed to darkness and light, who stand waiting by night and by dawn, holding cloaks and soft wrappings at the crossroads and gateways; they stand at the threshold, at the breaking of the paths, watching the lights, the rain and the winds, welcoming and farewelling our journeying souls. The price of such people is above rubies. No machines that go ping can stand in their place. Yet so often that is all we have. Thank God it doesn't happen to me.

I am fully dilated. O, the opening to the world. Full moon, the great roundness, O. I hear the obstetrician saying to the midwife, 'We can do this.' Inside I am singing. Joy. I hold tightly to my husband's hand. I am being covered in green sheets. The midwife apologises for them but I don't care: to me it is as though I am being decked out to meet the beloved, the creature who has squirmed inside me, the being to whom my heart and lungs and blood have been pledged for nine long months.

The room is filling with the moment. Everything seems to be leaning forward and swelling. My eyes keep flickering towards the crib and its soft wrappings. I have forgotten the machines, I no longer feel the straps, the drips, the rolls of tape on my thighs: they no longer bother me. To my mind at least, the instruments are quiet, like eyes in some spacecraft where the crew is watching, waiting for the unknown creature that has been sensed approaching. Stars, waiting, rolling, falling, darkness ... far, far away the giant white bear lumbers on the ice ...

In a mirror, I see my child's wet crown. The mirror wobbles away like water and I hear a sound like ... I don't know what ... I've never heard anything remotely like it, perhaps a kind of gurgle, a rattle ... I am at a loss, I think maybe someone has fainted ... I look swiftly around but no one is missing ... then with a shock I understand—it is the sound of a baby being turned in the birth canal and gently prised out. I must hold my breath if I am to push but after so many hours of the labouring rhythm I can't seem to get out of *a-pant-a-pant-a-pant-a-pant:* it has become like a reflex. The midwife has to hold my jaws shut as I give three of the greatest pushes of my life.

There is our wet babe curled upon my stomach, a big heavy long-limbed child I instantly recognise as *the one inside*. Our eyes feast and range over every part of the baby, checking, marvelling, recognising. Seeing this bonny big baby I understand everything—the kicks under the right rib, the squirms, the perpetual nine-month tummy aches, the ravenous hunger. I am happy just to feel the wet skin against mine, to accustom myself to the once-me-but-not-me sensation of flesh, fingers, hair, toes. All around me voices are laughing and praising, urging me to tell them the sex of the child but I am too mesmerised and confused to work out how to do it.

It is my husband who looks and shouts, 'It's a girl!'

Of course. A girl. I feel I have always known her, always, always my girl. 'So it's you,' I whisper. 'So it's you, Rebecca.'

My girl has two stains on her milky new face, two round marks where the forceps pulled her into the world. The tiny stains are beautiful in their precision: no more and no less than what was necessary. They are the work of a masterly feminine hand, like embroidery or the setting of diamonds. The sight of them fills me with gratitude and awe. They make my daughter's face more striking than any on the Sistine Chapel ceiling.

I am not the only one to admire my female doctor's skill: the midwives are openly impressed, especially as I have got away with only a small tear. It might be unfair but I am certain only a woman could have been so careful, so delicate. It's hard to describe the love you feel for the deliverer of your child; it's not just gratitude to be relieved from pain or harm but the feelings, very rare in life, that you have been completely seen. The woman in labour and her midwife are an ancient couple; with the advent of the male obstetrician, the relationship between this pair has been made into a syndrome, something of a well-known joke, but it does not change the fact that it is real and powerful. To bring a human being into the world involves emotion, not just veterinary science. I have so much love for the attendant women who have worked with my husband and me on our harvest day.

My daughter sleeps in her father's arms. They lie curled in a bed across the ward from me. Like my mother before me, I am too exhausted to hold my daughter, to explore, cuddle and feed. At least in this generation, I suckled her briefly before I collapsed. At least in this generation I can see my baby nearby through my half-closed eyes, see her cradled in the arms of my other self and know that her first hours were flesh-to-flesh with someone who loves her as fiercely as I do.

Rebecca.

Don't let anyone ever say that these first things, the way of entering the world, don't matter. They can be overcome, altered, repaired, healed, resented, suppressed, forgotten and

denied but they matter. Rebecca. Seeing her little face against
her father's turns me back into the bruised newborn of my
mother's and my lifelong myth. I feel myself in the efficient
swaddling of the nursery, tagged and alone under the
fluorescent light. Mamma sleeps down a long corridor, the
corridor of fear and pain, the longest corridor in the world.
We struggled and fought to reach each other over that
distance for years; I don't think my mother has ever got
over the way I was born. I never knew any better, until
now.

Rebecca.
Cold blue
You heave your first breaths to shore
Beached in milk shallows,
Shell-secret ears, seaweed fingers waving
Still stitched by liquid, your face is pinched
By puckers, the half-sobs that crawl
And scuttle across your ever-shifting
Blur of skin, as your limbs
Churn the deep dance of the tides

Air cuts your lungs dry
They fly, two birds in the desert sobbing
You claw upwards to them,
Splayed on the edge of this air-burning rim.
Thirst prises open your undersea eyes
Spilling in the blue blue tumult,

And now the heat of some vibrous love,
Some thick mammalian tremor rolls
You upwards

Uncorded, unravelled
You knead flesh through trembling flesh
Across the stinging spaces
Now the first of the billion breaths fly through you
Puffing you to the edge of daylight
As you climb, arms akimbo to the brown fruit moon
Mother, luminous, round
Swallowing at crater's edge the seeded waters
Hands clasped downwards murmuring
To the far forgotten echoes
The white unbroken shore forever inside
Lapping
Out

Taking her home is terrifying. Numb with exhaustion, stupefied from sleepless nights, crazy with love and rigid with fear, I struggle from day to night to day to night; the weeks become a blur. I am tied to her by an invisible cord: I leak milk at her every squawk. Her unhappiness drives me to despair, her suckling empties and fills me like the tides. When she sleeps and her face 'smiles with the angels' as my mother insists, I cry with happiness and wonder if I am going mad. I wait and watch through the heaviness of time with my beloved tormentor, growing her under the sun and the moon, weighing her plumpness and measuring her curled limbs.

Words are useless in this realm. All my life I've clutched at words, patted them, cultivated them, played with them, nodded seriously at the world of ideas and concepts. Now I have to release them, watch them disappear like a flock of birds into the air.

The world of the mother is silent, watchful, physical, here-and-now. Like all art, it looks like nothing. From the outside it seems as though anyone could do it. Yet it's a calling profound and consuming, with its rewards and punishments, its beauty and its hell. It ages women, humbles them, rents them apart, shakes marriages, confronts men with the spectre of their own tenderness and frailty. Every day in mansions and in one-roomed apartments, in starvation and in plenty, women are raising children. So what, says the world, so what? It's normal to fear for your milk, it's normal to be sleepless, it's normal to have dying babies in the third world, it's normal to have seventeen-year-old single mothers in boxy flats going around the bend, it's normal to rock a cradle, comfort, jiggle, sing, pat, kiss, bathe, tend, defend, worry and love so intensely your life can never be the same again even if you want it to be. Life itself is often a 'so what?' matter amongst us, invisible, interior, valueless. The mother is left at a loss for words, mute in the babble of politics and professions, wars and wages going on outside. The mother's world is the so-called art of the small. But the One Thousand and One Things outside are like nothing against the slightest movement in the universe of nurture. We practise that paradoxical art where a little at the right time is everything. The world doesn't deal in this currency.

I talk to my mother over the phone, incredulous that she could have done this three times. I apologise for being a bad baby, for never sleeping through the nights for five years, for screaming my head off for months on end, for foraging into cupboards, stairs, laundries, for being a real pain in the arse. My elderly mother's advice to me is 'things go forwards not backwards; every day she's growing older: think of all the pretty dresses you'll put on her ...'

No matter what my daughter does, to my mother it is never as bad as what I did as a baby. *Nonna* (grandmother) aligns with the baby, defending her colic and wakefulness against the naive mother who has yet to pay her dues. It's aggravating for me but at last my mother is free to enjoy babies, to revel in their little ways. It is pleasurable, even a relief, to feel this first grandchild healing over the scars of the frightening things my siblings and I unwittingly did to my new and isolated young parents.

Oh the nights of patting-and-rocking and rocking-and-patting. We come to know the sighs and breaths, the screams and whimpers, the pacings and jiggings of the night; we have stumbled on to the despairing secret society of mothers and fathers walking prams in the star-cold parks, driving through deserted city streets. The nights are heavy with the entangled dreams of babies and parents who snatch unsynchronised moments of sleep in the foggy exhaustion.

I used to watch stick-thin third world babies on the television news and think 'how terrible'; I used to watch courtroom sketches of men who had raped, murdered and tortured women and I would hate them to the point where I would have liked to hang them myself; I used to see the family photographs of abducted children desperately reproduced in newspapers and think, 'oh no, not again'.

I used to see all these things and think, well it's a terrible world and when people wake up to themselves/ Party X gets into government/social security improves/the recession ends/the suburbs get better services/criminals get rehabilitated etc etc, these terrible things won't assault our world.

Now I understand the young mother who told me about the time she was staring out the window of a bus with her baby boy on her lap. A derelict staggered onto the road screaming abuse at her and she was surprised to find tears in her eyes. In that moment she imagined him as somebody's child, somebody's tiny little loved or unloved child. The pain was overwhelming. Becoming a new mother means walking around seeing everybody with new eyes: mass murderers, dictators, torturers. It is astonishing to realise that everyone in the world was once new, wet, helpless and hungry, mouth straining for milk . . .

Now I can't watch news reports of starving dispossessed peoples and immediately think about world politics because half the time I am sitting with my own child at the breast. Seeing another woman unable to give her baby food is obscene. I know the cost of that and the feel of that in my body; it hits me physically, straight in the solar plexus. I'm not *thinking* anything, I am in tears. Tears.

My husband looks at me worriedly. Apparently it's the hormones. The books say it's the big change in hormones from pregnancy to lactation.

Yeah, the hormones. Women get so emotional at this time. I mean, it's only a matter of life and death.

Penelope Leach, *Breast Is Best*, Nursing Mothers, controlled crying, comp feeds, *The Australian Guide to Good Toys* . . . the feed-'em-formula-and-be-done-with-it school, the mammary - mafia - breastmilk - till - they're - four theory . . . dum-dums versus thumb-thumbs . . . cloth versus Cosies . . .

Ideas. Over the next few weeks I face a lot of ideas, theories, philosophies, beliefs. From this time on, ideas crawl over me like ants on jam. Yet the old certainties, the faith in the system that once supported me well enough have gone. Instinct will be my only defence against the barrage of theories and possibilities and advice, yet my instinct needs sharpening on the blade of experience. I have to make mistakes, I have to take risks. In order to care for my child I will do things I never believed in and never read about and don't understand. If they work, they are right. If not we will try something else and fast. We will lurch from moment to moment. Such a way of living is humbling for someone who used to want to know what was going to happen next, the self who believed, however vaguely, in good ways and bad ways of going about things.

I have come to hang onto the words of an older mother of teenagers who shrugs and says to me 'don't worry about good and bad, only love and what is necessary'.

I have always appeared to be more emotionally forthcoming than my husband. I leaped where he feared to tread. He weighs his words, I scatter them. When we saw our house, I knew it was the right one straight away: he wanted to think about it. I adopted each cat and dog of our menagerie on impulse: he had his reservations.

In the weeks before our child was born, my husband suffered a crisis of confidence. He lapsed into broody silences, he watched a lot of television, he wasn't interested in shopping for change tables or size 000 singlets. We had some tense conversations about his fears for himself as a father. I was placid, dreamy, confident, sure that once the baby was in my arms, it would all unfold as it should.

When our first child was born, I was tense, anxious, fretful and overwhelmed by my responsibilities, fearing for myself as a mother. David was placid, dreamy, confident, twirling the babe in his arms, bathing, changing nappies, wheeling the pram, sure that it was all unfolding as it should.

So much for the old certainties. So much for our old predictable life.

Anything can happen. Life must be responded to as it unfolds. Preconceptions, plans, beliefs just get in the way. We are in the middle of growing a mystery and therefore no one has the answers. Yet we need to sort out the chaos. My child is forcing me to become less judgemental, more cautious in drawing conclusions: over and over I have to admit 'that's the way it was today' and 'I don't know for sure but this seems more effective than that for now.' I am nurtured by the acceptance of other parents, their tact: we are all in the same small boat on the same great sea.

It frightens me to think I might have lived the rest of my life without knowing this humbling, extraordinary secret world: this milky furious love.

Notes on Contributors

Debra Adelaide is a writer, editor, researcher, and mother of two children. Her most recent book is *The Hotel Albatross* (Random House: 1995).

Anna Booth is a former trade union executive and is now Vice President of the Sydney Harbour Casino; she has two children.

Gabrielle Carey is a writer who has recently been lecturing in creative and professional writing. Her latest book is *The Borrowed Girl* (Picador: 1994), and she has a daughter and now a son.

Julie Clarke is a writer and journalist who lives in the Blue Mountains; she has two children.

Anna Maria Dell'oso has written stories, drama, opera libretti, essays and film criticism. She is the author of

Cats, Cradles and Chamomile Tea (Random House: 1989) and the novella, *The King of the Accordion* (New England Regional Art Museum: 1995); she lives in Sydney with her husband and two daughters.

Sara Dowse is the author of *West Block* (Penguin: 1983), *Silver City* (Penguin: 1984), *Schemetime* (Penguin: 1990), and most recently, *Sapphires* (Penguin: 1984); she is also one of the contributors to *Canberra Tales* (Penguin: 1988, recently republished). She has had five children and lives in Canberra, where she writes full time.

Noni Hazlehurst is an actor and presenter of television shows such as 'Playschool' and 'Better Homes and Gardens'. She has two sons and lives in the Blue Mountains.

Adele Horin writes a regular column for the *Sydney Morning Herald*, and she has two children.

Dorothy Johnston is the author of the novels *Tunnel Vision* (Hale & Iremonger: 1984), *Ruth* (Hale & Iremonger: 1986) and *Maralinga My Love* (McPhee Gribble: 1988). She has also had stories published in the collection *Canberra Tales* (Penguin: 1988). She has one son and one daughter.

Mary Moody is a writer, and the NSW presenter of ABC TV's 'Gardening Australia' program. She is a mother of four, and is also a grandmother.

Fiona Place has had stories and poems published in many

literary journals. Her novel *Cardboard* (Local Consumption Publications: 1989) won the National Book Council Award for new writers in 1990. She now has two babies.

Annette Stewart is a university lecturer and author of various critical articles on literature. She has a book forthcoming on the novelist Barbara Hanrahan; she has one daughter and lives in Sydney.

Pat Mamajun Torres is a writer, artist, storyteller and oral historian, from the Yawuru, Jabirr-Jabirr and Nyul-Nyul groups of the West Kimberley region, near Broome, WA. She is the mother of five children, and is presently writer-in-residence at Batchelor College, NT.

Monica Trapaga is a singer, actor and 'Playschool' presenter. She has written and recorded two albums for children, *Monica's Tea Party* and *Clap Your Hands*, and she has two children of her own.

Brenda Walker is a writer and also a lecturer at the University of Western Australia. Her first novel, *Crush* (FACP: 1991), won the TAG Hungerford Award in 1990; her latest novel is *One More River* (FACP: 1993) and she has also edited the fiction anthology *Risks* (FACP: 1996). She has one son.

Rachel Ward is an actor and writer. She has three children, and lives in Sydney.

Sue Woolfe is the author of the novel *Painted Woman*

(Allen & Unwin: 1991) and the play of the same name, and *Leaning Towards Infinity* (Random House: 1996); with Kate Grenville she also co-authored the book *Making Stories: How Ten Australian Novels Were Written* (Allen & Unwin: 1993). She has one daughter.